THE
FISHERMAN'S
ELECTRICAL MANUAL

THE
FISHERMAN'S
ELECTRICAL MANUAL

JOHN C. PAYNE

SHERIDAN HOUSE

This edition first published 2003 by
Sheridan House Inc.
145 Palisade Street,
Dobbs Ferry, NY 10522

Library of Congress Cataloging-In-Publication Data
Payne, John C.
    The fisherman's electrical manual / John C. Payne
       p. cm.
    Includes index.
    ISBN 1-57409-173-5 (alk. paper)
    1. Fishing boats—Electric equipment—Handbooks, manuals,
etc. I. Title.
SH452.9.B58P38 2003
623.8'503—dc21   2003007504

Printed in the United States of America

ISBN 1-57409-173-5

Designed by Keata Brewer

Contents

Foreword

John Payne may speak with an accent but whatever he says, the words are easy to understand. It's because he speaks the language every boat owner needs; clear and accurate information presented in simple sentences. He is never ahead of the reader and there aren't many people who are experts in marine electronics with that ability. Well, John Payne is such a fellow.

As the Editor of the *BoatU.S. Trailering Magazine*, I am well aware of the need for someone with practical hands-on experience who can speak to, rather than at boaters. Too many times, in too many books, a relatively simple solution to a boat's electrical trouble is lost forever in a sea of shoptalk and jargon that requires someone with an engineering degree to understand (I'm also convinced these are the same guys who write the "simple" directions to VCR and DVD operation).

The Fisherman's Electrical Manual is written for the person who wants to spend more time on the water than trying to learn the meaning of a sentence he or she has just read. This is because John Payne spends a lot of his time giving standing room only seminars or having one-on-one conversations with boaters about problems they are having or about ways to make an electrical system more safe and efficient. He speaks our language.

If there ever was a book to make the marine electrical system understandable, this is the book. If there ever was a book that will give every boat owner more confidence about how things work, this is it. If there ever was a book you'll want to carry with you on board, this is the one to have. Trailer boat owners and fishermen are going to be well-served by John Payne's common sense approach to "Anything Electric." This is a guy who knows his stuff and, best of all, can explain it in an easy to understand manner. Every reader of *The Fisherman's Electrical Manual* is going to become a more complete boater as a result. And that's good for all of us.

Pat Piper
Editor - *BoatU.S. Trailering Magazine*

THE
FISHERMAN'S
ELECTRICAL MANUAL

1

OUTBOARD ELECTRICS

INTRODUCTION TO OUTBOARD ENGINES

The modern outboard engine has become very complex. New and stringent emissions regulations and standards such as the EPA 2006 and CARB 2008 have lead to many hi-tech systems that include Variable Valve Timing and Lift Electronic Control (VITEC); programmed electronic fuel injection; digital CDI and inductive ignition systems; automatic electric choke systems; electronic multi-point variable-ratio oil injection lubrication systems; Engine Command (ECM) Systems with up to 18 sensor inputs and alternators up to 60 amps output. Systems also include electrical power trim systems, and comprehensive alarm and monitoring systems covering oil pressure, overheating, low oil level, over-revving and water in fuel. To properly service most modern outboards you need several specialist tools and technical manuals.

THE OUTBOARD STARTING CONTROL SYSTEM

When the key switch is turned on, a control voltage is supplied from the battery to the starter motor solenoid, and the ignition control (CDI unit or Power pack) system. This may be interlocked with a neutral safety switch and the stop circuit. When the solenoid closes, current is supplied to the starter motor which then rotates and engages. The engine rotates and the charging coil or magneto generates a voltage and supplies this to the ignition module. This is rectified to DC and stored in a capacitor (also called a condenser). A second trigger or pulsar coil generates a smaller voltage and feeds this to the ignition module to time or synchronize the spark. This switches or triggers an electronic switch which then releases the capacitor stored charge. The output feeds the primary side of the ignition coil. The secondary side of the coil transforms the voltage to a high voltage up to 50,000 volts. This high voltage goes to the spark plugs. The plugs spark to ignite the fuel and the expanding gases force the piston downwards.

THE OUTBOARD STARTER MOTOR

Outboard engine starter motors are of the inertia type and drive the flywheel ring gear. The starter motor develops the high torque that is required to turn over the engine against the high cylinder compression. The most common causes of starter motor problems are bad connections causing voltage drop. If the starter motor grinds over slowly or the solenoid clicks away without any starter rotation, check the main positive and the negative circuit connections. The main connections are those heavy cables that come from the battery and terminate on the outboard engine. How much battery capacity is required to start outboards? The answer is to install the outboard manufacturers' minimum recommendation, and a good baseline is up to 50 HP–450 CCA; up to 120 HP–500 CCA and up to 350 HP–600 CCA. If you use the battery for other equipment you will have to factor that in to the capacity calculations. See chapters 5 and 6 for more on starting batteries, and battery ratings (CCA, Ah etc).

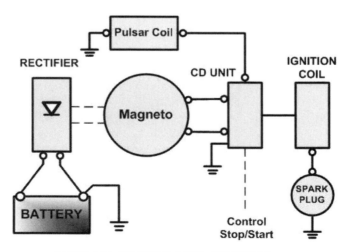

NISSAN OUTBOARD SYSTEM

TROUBLESHOOTING STARTER MOTOR SOLENOIDS

If the voltages at the main battery terminals and at the main solenoid input terminals are correct, check the solenoid. The solenoid is a large current capacity relay. Set the multimeter on the DC volts range and connect a probe on each of the two control coil connections. Turn the ignition key. There should be a voltage reading of 12–13 volts when the key is turned. If the voltage is correct and the solenoid does not operate the coil may have failed. If the solenoid clicks loudly, place a meter probe between the main negative terminal and the main output side of the solenoid. If a voltage is present the internal main contacts are good and voltage is being supplied to the starter motor. This indicates a possible starter motor problem.

OUTBOARD IGNITION CONTROL SYSTEMS

Electronic Control Modules (ECM) use capacitive discharge ignition (CDI) systems. The unit essentially has a capacitor which charges up and then discharges a high voltage to the primary input side of the coil. The CDI unit performs the switching that times the high voltage correctly for ignition. Computers or microprocessors are used to perform timing control and other functions. The control modules must be properly installed or premature failure will occur. Make sure the ground wires to the module chassis are attached and secure. Faults are often typified by reduced engine speeds and a failure to start.

ABOUT THE IGNITION COIL

The coil transforms the primary input of 12 volts to a secondary one of up to 50,000 volts for ignition. Coils are very reliable, and terminals should be checked and tightened. They must be kept clean to prevent tracking and loss of voltage. Erratic engine operation occurs when excessive moisture is present, causing surface voltage tracking to ground.

WHAT THE DISTRIBUTOR DOES

Older motors may have a distributor to "distribute" the high voltage via a rotor and breaker points to each cylinder ignition cable contact. A condenser is connected to the point circuit. The rotor is driven from the engine, and the cylinder-firing order is determined by the sequence in which the cables are inserted in the distributor. The points and condenser can be replaced with electronic ignition kits. Distributor caps should be clean and dry, and inspected for tracking, both internal and external to each high voltage contact point. Check that all gaskets and seals are in good condition and replace if degraded. The terminals often develop a "crust," that can be simply scraped off. Tracking, particularly in wet conditions, may cause misfiring and erratic engine operation.

ABOUT THE IGNITION CABLES

The ignition cables carry the high voltage to the spark plugs. Ignition cables degrade over time, and should be kept clean and dry. When the insulation cracks, tracking and grounding occur. The rubber boots or covers over the connections should be clean and seal well. Vibration also causes problems and the cables should be inspected for fatigue and cracking. Rough running is often caused by spark plug cable problems.

HOW SPARK PLUGS WORK

The spark plug carries the high voltage into the cylinder and ignites the fuel. It is important to clean and check spark plugs regularly. The spark gaps should be measured and adjusted to the correct clearance. The exterior ceramic or porcelain insulation must also be kept clean to prevent tracking to ground and reducing the ignition voltage. Many choose to replace spark plugs each season to avoid problems. Plug lead connections should be checked for corrosion and tightness. The main causes of spark plug problems are incorrectly set gaps or carbon fouling which short circuits the plug to ground. If you run for extended periods at slow outboard speeds, the spark plug electrode erosion will increase, and there will be increased deposits of carbon powder. Once the gap erodes to around 0.040 the motor will start misfiring, idle badly and have trouble starting. Slow speed running requires regular cleaning and adjustment. If spark plug gaps are too close the reduced spark will not ignite the fuel properly. If it is too large the voltage will not be able to arc across and create the spark that ignites the fuel. They must be set correctly.

CAUSES OF WEAK SPARK VOLTAGES

Causes of weak spark voltages include a failing magneto coil; clearance problems with magnets on the flywheel; connection problems from the magneto to the coil, or a loose ground connection. The battery charge level does not affect the ignition; if the engine starts, the ignition voltage is being supplied from the magneto.

TROUBLESHOOTING THE SPARKPLUGS

If the outboard engine will not start after checking voltages and connections, check the spark plugs.

Plug Color	Possible Cause
Golden or light brown	Good
Damp with fuel	No ignition, spark failure
Dry	No fuel
Black/carbonized	Fuel rich mixture Weak spark/ignition loss Oil mix in fuel wrong Wrong plug types

WHAT IS IGNITION PROTECTION?

All equipment in gasoline engines must be ignition protected under mandatory laws (i.e. USCG). Equipment may include alternators, starters, blowers, bilge pumps etc. Look at the nameplate or ratings data on the item for the IGN or Ignition Protected identification, or a UL rating statement. Starters and alternators that are not of correct design and ignition protection, or have been improperly rebuilt or assembled, can start an explosion.

THE IGNITION CONTROL SWITCH

The ignition switch comes in many variations depending on the outboard type. In many cases it is a simple 3-position switch. The switch positions are generally: Position 1 = Off. This disables the ignition circuit by grounding out the circuit. Position 2 = On. This supplies positive voltage to the ignition circuit and power to the accessories. Position 3 = Start. This is a spring return momentary contact position. When the contacts are made it supplies power to the solenoid and starter motor operation. What do the keyswitch letters mean? Letter B is the battery positive; letter A is the auxiliary or accessory supply; letter C is the choke position; letter S is the starter solenoid supply position; letter G is the ground connection and letter M is the magneto kill wire.

ABOUT MULTI-POSITION IGNITION SWITCHES

Many outboards have 3- or 4-position On-Off-Start-accessories switches, and these are found on many older models. In these switches there are two to three active switch positions. The switching arrangement provides electrical power to multiple circuits, as well as a grounding circuit for magneto return voltages. These switches may also have a push-to-choke position which is common on newer models such as Mercury outboards. The push-to-choke feature eliminates the requirement for a separate choke switch.

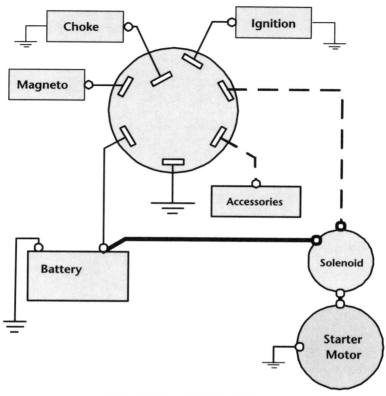

**TYPICAL OUTBOARD
ENGINE STARTING CIRCUIT**

Mercury/Mariner Outboard Wiring Color Code

Color	Circuit Function
Yellow/red	Starting circuits
Brown/yellow	Bilge blowers
Dark grey	Navigation light tachometer
Orange	Anode electrode mercathode
Brown	Reference electrode mercathode
Purple	Instruments
Dark blue	Oil pressure
Tan	Water temperature
Pink	Fuel gauge sender
Black	All grounds
Light blue/white stripe	Trim up switch
Light green/white stripe	Trim down switch
Brown/white stripe	Trim sender to trim gauge
Purple/white stripe	Trim "trailer" switch
Gray	Tachometer signal
Black/yellow stripe	Shorting or stop circuit
Pink	Fuel sender to gauge
Red	Unprotected wire from battery
Red/purple stripe	Protected (fused) wire from battery
Red/purple stripe	12 volt+ to trim panel control
Purple	Ignition switch to 12 volt +
Tan	Temp switch to warning horn
Tan	Temp sender to temp gauge

Tan/blue stripe	Temp switch to warning horn
Yellow	Starter solenoid to starter motor
Yellow	Starter to regulator (charging)
Yellow/red stripe	Start switch to start solenoid to neutral start switch
Yellow/black stripe	Choke (enrichener system)
Green with color stripe	Switch box to coil—striped and numbered
White/black stripe	Bias circuit (switch boxes)
Yellow/red	Ignition switch to solenoid
Brown/yellow	Bilge blowers
Dark grey	Navigation lights/tachometer
Orange	Accessory feeds
Brown	Pumps, alternator charge light
Purple	Instruments, supply ignition switch
Dark blue	Oil pressure
Tan	Water temperature—overheat
Pink	Fuel gauge sender
Red	Supply no fuse battery
Light blue/white	Trim up
Green/white	Trim down

ABYC Color Code Recommendations

Color	Circuit Function
Yellow/red	Ignition switch to solenoid
Brown/yellow	Bilge blowers
Dark grey	Navigation lights/tachometer
Orange	Accessory feeds
Brown	Pumps, alternator charge light
Purple	Instruments, supply ignition switch
Dark blue	Oil pressure
Tan	Water tempreaature—overheat
Pink	Fuel gauge sender
Red	Supply no fuse battery
Light blue/white	Trim up
Green/white	Trim down

OUTBOARD CHARGING SYSTEMS

There are often two coils, one for the magneto or ignition system, the other often called the charging or lighting coil for charging the battery. They have various ratings, the larger the engine the larger the output. Ratings of 40 amps (504 watts) with dual voltage regulators and 20 amps (252 watts) are on larger motors. The correct charging voltage will be in the range of 14 to 14.5 volts. New high output alternators such as those on larger Honda outboards are rated at 60 amps and are belt driven. Alternators are now being designed for low speed charging characteristics which suits trolling. Some 12-amp Honda units output 10 amps at just 2000 rpm. It is important to note that quoted maximum charging outputs are rated for cold engines, and when charging coils are hot the charging output reduces.

WHAT IS THE STATOR?

The stator is the fixed winding that creates an electromagnetic field. It supplies alternating current (AC) to the rectifier.

WHAT IS THE ROTOR?

The rotor is the rotating part of the alternator. In an outboard engine rotors are magnets fixed to the flywheel, and can number up to 12. They rotate through the field created by the stator winding.

WHAT IS THE RECTIFIER?

The rectifier or diode block consists of a network of diodes. One diode is connected to the positive side, and one to the negative side. The positive half waves pass through the positive side diodes and the negative half waves pass through the negative diodes. This rectifies the generated AC phase voltages into the DC output used for battery charging.

WHAT IS THE VOLTAGE REGULATOR?

The charging coil output is passed through a voltage regulator. The regulator maintains a stable voltage at all times throughout the speed range of the outboard engine.

TWIN OUTBOARD CHARGING SYSTEMS

When two outboard engine charging systems feed one battery bank, generally one will burn out a stator coil. It is better to maintain each circuit separately and have an emergency switch to connect both starting batteries. There are a range of switch configurations available. Mistakes occur easily and both batteries can get drained down. It is also easy to turn off a switch or parallel both engine charging systems and damage the alternators.

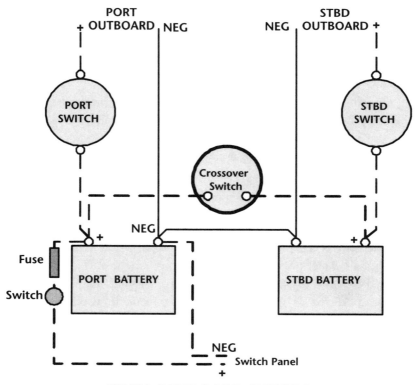

TWIN OUTBOARD SYSTEM

SINGLE ENGINE CHARGING - DUAL BATTERIES

When a remote isolator such as a ProXtra, Hellroarer or Battery Bank Integrator unit is used, the initial charging goes to the start battery. When the charging voltage rises to 13.4 volts, the isolator switches on and diverts charging current to the deep cycle house or trolling motor battery. The isolator has very low resistance so a full charge voltage is supplied for charging.

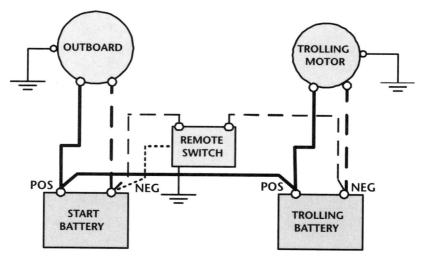

SINGLE ENGINE CIRCUIT DIAGRAM

ABOUT STOP AND NEUTRAL POSITION CIRCUITS

The stop circuits within multi-position ignition switches or in lanyard type emergency stop switches are a constant cause of problems and start failures. In normal operation the contacts are open, and close to shut-down. Some engines may have a tilt-stop switch that activates when the engine is tilted too far up, a common occurrence when fishing in shallows. If the engine control is not in neutral position the engine will not start. In many cases a faulty switch or a failure to activate will be the cause of non-starting. The neutral position switches within throttle controls can work loose, be out of adjustment or just mechanically fail. Move the throttle forward and reverse in and out of the center position.

ABOUT CHARGING SYSTEM FAULTS AND FAILURES

The most common cause of charging system faults are:

- **Reverse Polarity Connection.** This is a common cause of rectifier failure. Reversal of the positive and negative leads will destroy the rectifier diodes.
- **Open Circuit Operation.** If the engine is run with the charging coil not connected to a battery the diode rectifier may be damaged. If a switch in charging system is opened the same will occur.
- **Short Circuiting Positive and Negative.** A short circuit will cause excess current to be drawn through the diodes and the subsequent failure of one or more of diodes. The most common cause is reversing the battery connections.
- **Winding Failures.** Stator winding failures are usually caused by overloading and overheating. This is normally due to insufficient ventilation at long term high output causing insulation failure.

ABOUT INSTRUMENTATION SYSTEMS

Most boats have engine tachometers, oil pressure and water temperature gauges, volts and ammeters. Mercury, Mariner, Suzuki, Yamaha, Honda, Tohatsu, OMC, and others have systems that are similar although wiring colors may vary. The most common faults are caused by bad connections at the sensor or gauge, and loss of the negative. Another common fault is the use of Teflon thread tape or pipe sealant on the sender unit threads in the engine. This stops the sender grounding.

ABOUT OUTBOARD TACHOMETERS

The sender input signal comes from different sources depending on the outboard type. The alternator output is common on 2- and 4-cycle outboards with 4, 6, 8, 10 and 12 magnetic pole alternators. These tachometer inputs go to one of the two alternator wires to the rectifier, to pick up the AC pulse. Evinrude, Johnson (gray wire) connects to alternator connection on powerhead, and not the ignition.

Mariner/Mercury (gray wire) connects to alternator connection or rectifier on powerhead, and not the ignition. Honda (gray, gray/yellow wire) black/yellow connects to ignition. Suzuki (yellow) connects to terminal in powerhead. Tohatsu (yellow, yellow/gray wire) connects to terminal in powerhead. Yamaha (green wire) connects to terminal in powerhead. All wiring must be fastened clear of hot or moving parts. The range selector must be set correctly. When power is turned on the gauge should read zero. If it does not, make sure the ignition (IGN) and ground (GND) are not incorrectly connected. IGN to GND voltage should read 12–16 volts. If the gauge does not follow RPM this may indicate a faulty rectifier (a diode failure). When the reading is too high or low the range switch may be set wrong. Check tachometer signal at the gauge using meter set on AC and speed of 2000 rpm. You should get 3–7 volts AC. Check and make sure all ground connections are clean and tight.

TROUBLESHOOTING INSTRUMENT SYSTEMS

Open Sensor Test. Take off the sensor lead marked "SEND" or "G" from the rear of the gauge. Switch on the ignition meter supply voltage. The gauge needle should be as follows with infinite resistance:

- Temperature Gauge—full left-hand position.
- Pressure Gauge—full left-hand position.
- Tank Gauge—full left-hand position.
- Trim Gauge—Mercury/Mariner full RH position.
- Trim Gauge—Evinrude/Johnson full LH position.

Sensor Ground Test. This test shorts out the sensor input terminal "SEND" or "G" to negative (GND). The sensor lead must be removed and the meter power supply on. The gauge needle should be as follows with no resistance:

- Temperature Gauge—full right-hand position.
- Pressure Gauge—full right-hand position.
- Tank Gauge—full right-hand position.
- Trim Gauge—Mercury/Mariner full LH position.
- Trim Gauge—Evinrude/Johnson full RH position.

Sensor Testing. Disconnect the cables, and use a multimeter on the resistance range. Place the positive (red) meter probe on the terminal marked "SEND" or "G" on sensor. Place the negative (black) meter probe on the sensor thread. Resistance ranges vary, and auto systems may be in the 10–120 ohm range.

- **Temperature Sensors.** Readings should be in the range at 25°C of 240–33 ohms.
- **Pressure Sensors.** Readings should be: High Pressure = 33 ohms. Half pressure = 103 ohms. Low (Zero) Pressure = 240 ohms.
- **Fuel Tank Sensors.** Reading should be: Empty = 240 ohms. Half = 103 ohms. Full = 33 ohms.
- **Trim Senders.** Resistance ranges between engines OMC/ Johnson (1–188 ohms), Mercury (10–167 ohms), Yamaha (411–110 ohms). Up = 1 to 411 ohms. Down = 5 to 240 ohms.

ABOUT FUEL MONITORING SYSTEMS

The FloScan fuel monitor has an opto-electronic turbine flow transducer. The rotor in the fuel line rotates with the fuel flow. The turning rotor interrupts an infrared light beam between an LED and phototransistor to count the rotations. The faster the flow, the higher the count. This pulsed signal is processed by the monitor microprocessor, computing gph (l/hr), fuel consumed, etc. The flow sensor is installed between the fuel tank and priming bulb. A tacho input may also be used. Make sure all sensor input connections are tight, clean and dry. Both grounds and positive DC inputs must be secure.

HYDRAULIC POWER TILT AND TRIM SYSTEMS

Regular system checks must be made. Tilt the motor up and engage the tilt support. Take off the filler cap and check the fluid level. If required add the recommended fluid to bring the level to the bottom of the fill cap hole when at the full tilt position. Slow cycling is often caused by voltage drops in bad switch contacts or motor connections. The motor can also be a problem, as well as seized bearings or worn or sticking brushes.

2

TROLLING MOTORS

ABOUT TROLLING MOTORS

Trolling motors have revolutionized fishing, in particular for bass and walleye. They are used to slowly and quietly hold position or troll along drop-offs and weed lines, zigzag along weed beds, or slow the drift rate against wind, waves and currents. They come in a variety of configurations, with bow mount and transom mount. Motorguide and Minn Kota are the main manufacturers.

HOW TO SELECT A TROLLING MOTOR

There are a number of considerations when selecting a trolling motor. Should it be bow or stern mounted? Fishing boats do not generally travel in a straight line. It is easier to pull a boat along rather than push it, and easier to move a bow rather than a stern around. The bow mounted motor is most common as it gives greater control, faster response and more precise positioning. It uses less thrust and less power. What about the control? Hand tiller, foot switch, hand or laser wireless. Voltage and thrust rating are described in later chapters.

CHOOSING SHAFT LENGTHS

There is a standard requirement for 18 inches of the shaft in the water when the motor is down. Minn Kota recommend 36 inches where the deck to water clearance is 10-16 ; 42 inches for 16-22 inch clearance, 45-52 inches for 22-28, and 54-62 inches for 28-34. Where rougher water conditions are likely, an additional 5 inches is added to the length. This is to prevent cavitation when the prop lifts out of the water.

WHAT DOES THE TERM THRUST MEAN?

Trolling motors are specified in terms of the thrust output capability. It is the thrust and not the output of the electric motor in kW or HP that determines effectiveness. Thrust is a static measurement of force. It is a result of the power developed by the electric motor, the propeller shape, pitch and dimensions, and the speed in rev/min. Trolling motors have props designed to achieve maximum acceleration for immediate response. There is no precise correlation between thrust and horsepower.

HOW MUCH THRUST IS REQUIRED?

The general rule of thumb in choosing the required thrust is to take the total weight of the loaded boat and divide it by 70. For example, if your boat with people and gear weighs a total of 3500 lbs (1700 kg) you divide this by 70. That means that a motor with at least 50 lbs of thrust is required. Another method is 5 lbs thrust for every 200–350 lbs of boat weight. Depending on your fishing the wind and current should be factored in. Since the draft of a boat affects the drift rate, shallow draft or high freeboard cabin type fishing boats tend to have a greater wind (sail plane) effect than deeper draft low freeboard. Greater thrust will be required with strong river or tidal flows.

HOW MUCH POWER DO MOTORS USE?

The general rating is 1.2 amps per pound of thrust for 12-volt systems, 0.85 amp per pound in 24-volt systems, and 0.5 amp per pound for 36-volt systems. You should verify this with your motor manufacturers' data.

Typical Trolling Motor Data

Motor Thrust	Current A/V	Boat Length	Total Boat Weight
24 lbs	27A/12V	12–14 ft	1950 lbs
30 lbs	30A/12V	12–14 ft	2100 lbs
36 lbs	36A/12V	12–14 ft	2520 lbs
40 lbs	40A/12V	14–15 ft	2800 lbs
42 lbs	40A/12V	14–15 ft	2940 lbs
45 lbs	40A/12V	15–16 ft	3080 lbs
48 lbs	40A/12V	15–16 ft	3360 lbs
50 lbs	40A/12V	16–18 ft	3500 lbs
55 lbs	45A/12V	16–18 ft	3850 lbs
65 lbs	38A/24V	18–19 ft	4550 lbs
74 lbs	50A/24V	20–21 ft	5180 lbs
82 lbs	50A/24V	20–21 ft	6000 lbs
101 lbs	37A/36V	22+ ft	7070 lbs
107 lbs	40A/36V	22+ ft	7200 lbs
109 lbs	42A/36V	22+ ft	7300 lbs
130 lbs	76A/24V	22+ ft	7500 lbs

WHICH VOLTAGE IS THE BEST TO SELECT?

Boats generally have 12-volt systems, so installing a 12-volt trolling motor is logical and simple. The advantages of 24- and 36-volt motors are that the size may be reduced. Power is also increased for the same physical size, and the supply cable sizes reduced. The motors will operate more efficiently with reduced voltage drop problems. This requires more batteries, and in some cases the installation of series switching.

ABOUT CHOOSING TROLLING BATTERY CAPACITY

Battery principles are covered in Chapter 5. For example, a 55-lb thrust motor unit that takes 40 amps is installed. Each use period will be 6 hours at average half load of 20 amps. This means that the motor will require a battery load of 120 Ah. A battery bank rated at 240 Ah capacity is selected so that deep cycling is to 50%. Ideally the nominal rating of the battery bank will be 20 amps at the 10-hour rate. If the trolling motor is used at higher average levels, i.e. 30 or 40 amps, the actual available battery capacity will be reduced 10–15% or more. This is called Peukerts Coefficient. Always select a battery bank rated at the 10-hour rate if possible. This will match the trolling motor current requirement as close as possible to the battery characteristics while you are fishing.

HOW DOES A TROLLING MOTOR WORK?

Trolling motors are either permanent magnet or brush type DC motors. The permanent magnet motor has permanent magnets in place of the traditional DC motor pole shoes and excitation windings. The advantages are significant reductions in size and weight, greater efficiency and no maintenance. Traditional DC motors have field wound rotors, with larger brushes and commutators to reduce heat build-up. Do not run the motor out of the water except for very short periods as there is no water to transfer the heat out of the motor casing.

HOW DOES SPEED CONTROL WORK?

Speed control was carried out on early model motors using resistors and speed coils. These were switched in and out of circuit by connecting them in series with the motor. This reduced the voltage to the motor by absorbing power in the coils, and therefore the speed was lowered. Speed coils generate heat that has to be dissipated and is quite inefficient. Speed coils are located in the lower motor housing and the excess heat is dissipated through the housing to the water. The speed control knob is mounted on the foot pedal. The speed range varies from zero to 100% on the standard setting, with a fine speed adjustment having a 10% range.

CONVERTING FROM 12 TO 24/36 VOLT SYSTEM

Many fishermen end up converting from a 12-volt trolling motor to a 24- or 36-volt motor. This creates a few technical difficulties. The outboard is generally 12 volts along with the charging system. In most cases there is a dedicated trolling motor battery bank, which is recharged at the end of each day or fishing trip. The outboard is 12 volts and has a dedicated start battery. Some fishermen will install 1 or 2 extra batteries and use the start battery to make up the voltage, but I do not recommend this. Always keep your start battery separate. With a 24/36 volt trolling motor system it is common to tap the 12-volt boat supply circuits off one of the series connected batteries. If possible it is better to split the loads into 2 or 3 to balance this. If connected across one battery, it is good practice to rotate to each battery. This means changing the connection to the next battery each trip.

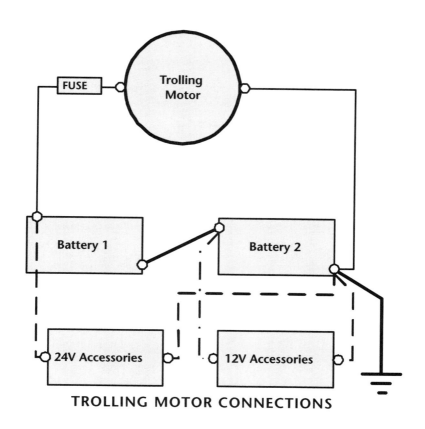

TROLLING MOTOR CONNECTIONS

WHAT IS PWM SPEED CONTROL?

The Pulse Width Modulated (PWM) system uses transistors that are rapidly switched on and off, or pulsed. The Motorguide DuraAmp and the Minn Kota Maximizer switch on and off at around 20,000–30,000 times per second. The transistor switch on/off times are controlled and the current flow level is dependent on the ratio between the on and off periods. The larger the ratio the more current will flow. The lower the ratio the less current will flow. This variable on/off ratio gives a square wave. The PWM is a much more efficient system than dropping resistors or coils. The pulses reach full voltage and produce greater motor torque. The only disadvantage is that electrical interference is generated. As all motors at switch on with load take quite large currents, the Maximizer has a soft start feature which limits the motor speed at start up so it is smooth. This helps extend motor life. The illustration shows the basic arrangement for a modern system.

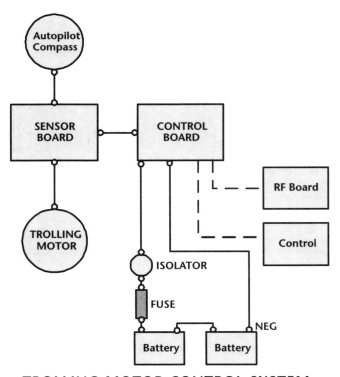

TROLLING MOTOR CONTROL SYSTEM

HOW TO CALCULATE CABLE SIZES

The efficiency of trolling motors is directly related to the battery supply voltage levels, the available battery capacity, and the voltage drop
in the supply cables during operation. There is no standardized wiring
size as each installation can vary. Some recommendations call for a 6
or 8 AWG cable for boats of 18 ft and up. When it comes to the
trolling motor I recommend aiming for the minimum volt drop possible, which maximizes motor efficiency and running times. The basic
questions to be answered are:

1. How much current in amps will the motor draw?
2. What is the total cable distance from the battery positive to the
   motor and back to the battery negative? In DC circuits both
   positive and negative must be considered. The shorter the run
   the better, so locate batteries as close as possible to the motor.
3. What size of cable will match the motor current?
4. How much voltage drop in the motor circuit will there be at
   the rated current and cable size? Some recommend using a voltage loss chart or curves to determine voltage loss per foot. I
   have made up a simple chart based on this. The alternative is to
   calculate the voltage drop precisely.
5. It is important to factor in other points of resistance that cause
   voltage drops. Selection of the next cable size up compensates
   for this. In a series circuit all resistances are added together. R1
   (Battery Connection) + R2 (Positive Cable) + R3 (Control
   Unit or Speed Switch Unit) + R4 (Positive Motor Connection)
   + R5 (Negative Motor Connection) + R6 (Negative Cable) +
   R7 (Negative Battery Connection) = R (Total).

Volt Drop per Foot Table

AWG/mm	20A	30A	40A	50A
4/25	.0005V	.0075V	.01V	.0125V
6/16	.008V	.012V	.016V	.020V
8/10	.0128V	.0192V	.0256V	.032V
10/6	.0204V	.0306V	.0408V	.051V
12/4	.0324V	.0486V	.0648V	.081V

Example. For maximum 5% voltage drop at 12.5 volts (.625Volt).

1. The trolling motor is rated at 40 amps.
2. The total cable distance is 20 feet forward multiplied by 2. This equals 40 feet.
3. Start with 10 AWG. Check the table across for 40 amps.
4. The volt drop is given as .0408 volt per foot.
5. Multiply 40 x .0408 = 1.632 volts. This is unacceptable.
6. Retry with 4 AWG. The volt drop is given as .01 volt per foot.
7. Multiply 40 x .01 = 0.4 volt. This is acceptable.

USING THE CHART BASED CALCULATION METHOD

If the same circuit numbers of 40 amps over 40 feet are used the volt drop table at 3% requires the next cable size up. This is the better choice that will give you the best performance.

3% Voltage Drop Table

	40 ft	35 ft	30ft	25 ft
80A	0 AWG	0 AWG	1 AWG	2 AWG
70A	1 AWG	1 AWG	2 AWG	2 AWG
60A	1 AWG	2 AWG	2 AWG	2 AWG
50A	2 AWG	2 AWG	2 AWG	4 AWG
40A	2 AWG	2 AWG	4 AWG	4 AWG
30A	4 AWG	4 AWG	4 AWG	6 AWG
20A	6 AWG	6 AWG	6 AWG	8 AWG

INSTALLING THE CIRCUIT PROTECTION

In most cases the trolling motor will be rated much less than the supply cable. Motorguide recommend a 50A fuse or circuit breaker. A circuit breaker 15% above rated motor current or a slow blow fuse should be sufficient. Slow Blow fuses are used as the fluctuating loads must not cause fuse failure in normal service. The fuse must be located as close as possible to the battery, ideally within 12–18 inches or less.

WHAT IS SERIES SWITCHING?

When trolling motors are 24- or 36-volt powered, it may be necessary to connect two batteries in series for 24 volts, or three to get 36 volts. This can be done automatically, using a series and parallel relay. In normal mode the batteries are connected in parallel to supply boat power. When the trolling motor is activated the batteries are disconnected from the parallel and reconnected in series. When the switch is turned off they return to parallel. A separate battery is recommended. Disconnect trolling motor from the batteries before charging. Simply open the battery isolator. Always open the isolator when clearing the propeller, or when the motor is not in use.

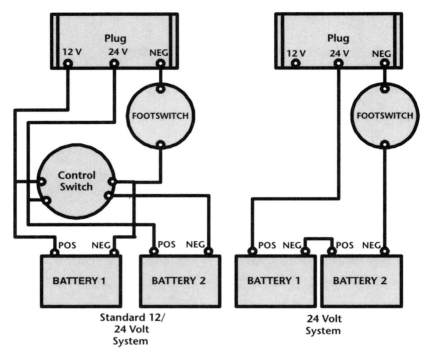

TROLLING MOTOR POWER SYSTEM

TROLLING MOTOR POWER SUPPLY SOCKETS

Many trolling motors have plugs and sockets, with watertight sealing caps. These are often dual voltage 12/24 outputs. They must be kept clean and dry to avoid high resistance, overheating and burn-outs. Always unplug the trolling motor or switch it off at the battery when not in use. One of the common problems is switch and footswitch burnouts. These often have large volt drops across the contacts which reduces available power to the trolling motor. There are a variety of methods to modify these circuits. The modifications are similar to systems for anchor winches, which use a main high current circuit solenoid with a separate control circuit. The solenoid switching is inserted in the negative side of the circuit.

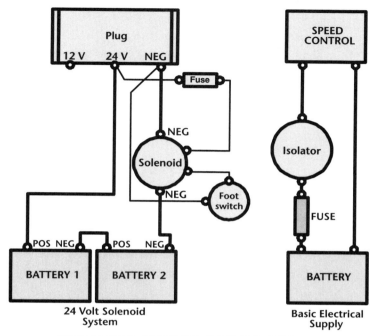

TROLLING MOTOR POWER SYSTEM

HOW DOES POWER STEERING WORK?

Some units have autopilot power steering. It locks on to the required course, and has a small fluxgate compass. The heading angle stability is within 2 degrees and maintains this against wind, tide and current. Some units can now be connected to the sounder unit, and use the depth data to track a bottom contour, channel or shoreline.

HOW DOES THE POWER STOW FUNCTION WORK?

A foot pedal is used to automatically lower the motor into the water. The stow button will raise the motor back up. A small motor is used and most problems will be bad connections. If the unit operates slowly, and voltage is correct at the drive motor terminals, the unit may be binding and overloading the motor.

WHAT IS POWER TRIM?

The power trim feature is used to adjust the depth of motor for sneaking inshore in shallow waters. This minimizes the chances of touching the bottom and damaging the propeller and shaft. The circuit uses a small electric motor. The main problems are bad connections. If the unit operates slowly, and voltage is correct at the drive motor terminals the motor may be mechanically binding.

WHAT ARE POWER METERS USED FOR?

Some trolling motors have a real time battery gauge that displays the hours running time left at the current speed setting. The meters have a small ammeter shunt that monitors the current. This is input to a processor for calculation against a timer and then shown on the LED display.

WHAT CAUSES TROLLING MOTOR INTERFERENCE?

Interference often occurs on fish finders and GPS. This is caused by some trolling motor pulse width modulation (PWM) speed control systems. Some LCD displays may go to a solid black, or just blank out. Flasher type sounders may stop flashing. It is more common on trolling motor mounted transducers. The interference really depends on the make and type of sounder, where it is located, where the transducer is installed, and how the wiring is installed. The worst cases appear to be when fishfinders are set in manual mode with high gain or sensitivity settings, and low speed motor operation. The most common error is the fastening of the transducer cable to power cable or the foot pedal assembly cable.

HOW TO TRACK DOWN THE NOISE SOURCES

It is best to do a noise check on all boats. Operate all equipment, bilge pumps, trolling motors, bait livewell aerator pumps, power tilt and trim control, tachometers, fish finders (with sensitivity set to 75%). If noise or interference is observed, systematically switch each item off until the noise disappears. Sometimes two or more pieces of equipment may have relatively low noise levels but be cumulative. If the trolling motor is found to be the cause, place the motor in the high by-pass mode. This will usually stop the noise. Bad wiring is not usually the cause.

HOW TO STOP TROLLING MOTOR INTERFERENCE

If the cause is found to be the trolling motor there are several remedies to consider. The first is the connection of the trolling motor. The supply wiring should go directly to the battery, and in some cases if electronics are connected they may have to be connected to another battery. The second solution is the routing of the supply cables. The motor cables should be installed as far as possible from other wiring, preferably on the opposite side of the boat. The transducer wiring should not be too close to trolling motor wiring. In severe cases the transducer may have to be moved to a new location. If the boat is fiberglass the internal transducer relocation is relatively easy. In some cases the fishfinder power supply may have to be connected directly to the outboard cranking battery. Depending on where the transducer is, the cables should be installed and strapped to the outside of the trolling motor. The transducer cable should not be fastened in the control loom from the footswitch or power supply. Motorguide have an RF choke available. The sonar cable is wrapped 5 turns around half of the clam-shell RF choke. This should be as close as possible to the sonar and it filters out noise to the sonar. On many boats, accessories and forward mounted sounders are powered off the trolling motor batteries. The grounds and negatives must all be held at the same level to reduce noise. Pinpoint have developed a range of interference-free 20° puck transducers. The patented pending design shields the transducer from electrical noise generated within PWM speed controls.

GROUNDING TROLLING MOTORS

The motor must be grounded to the boat's common ground. If ungrounded, interference levels may be higher and also may increase corrosion. The ground of the small boat is to the negative side of the battery. The ground jumper is connected from the negative to the casing inside the pedal assembly on the Motorguide Tour Edition. In the

36-volt units an additional cable is installed back to the battery negative. In hand operated models an additional cable is fastened to the upper shaft with a hose clamp and taken back to the battery negative. It is best to solder bare for about 1 inch, and fold it once before inserting it under the clamp. Cover with self-amalgamating tape to protect from weather.

WHAT MAINTENANCE IS REQUIRED?

Keep motors clean and dry when not in use. In saltwater estuaries all salt must be washed off. Sacrificial zinc or anodes on a saltwater model shaft must be monitored and replaced if required. Make sure that the surfaces are clean. It is good practice to remove and refasten regularly. The zinc must be fastened just above the lower unit. If the trolling motor gets a season of hard use, get the motor checked and vacuum out all carbon dust. Nothing wrecks commutator condition or causes sparking more than excess dust deposits. The dust can seize brushes in brush-holders. The key to DC motor life is regular maintenance.

TROUBLESHOOTING TROLLING MOTORS

The motor power is lower than normal: Be careful when you use your motor while fishing in thick vegetation. If the vegetation wraps around the prop it will cause overloads and higher currents. The high currents cause general overheating which affects all parts of the motor. Check for low battery voltages and for loose cable connections that cause resistance and loss of power.

The motor has lost power: Where the power is supplied from clip connection, check that the connections are secure and not corroded. Check that the battery voltage has not fallen. With a new installation, check that wire sizes are large enough. Make sure that all connections are secure, dry and not corroded. The permanent magnet may have cracked or be chipped, although this happens rarely. The motor also may make whining or grinding noises. There may be water in the lower unit.

The motor will not operate at any speed: Reset the manual reset circuit breaker in the trolling motor. Check supply fuse or circuit breaker.

Check all battery and circuit connections, plugs, sockets and switches for corrosion, loose terminals. Check all control and bypass switches for loose connections. Rotate the propeller by hand and verify it is free. Binding or resistance indicates that motor magnets may be chipped or loose.

The motor has lost one or more speeds: Check for loose connections in the speed switch and potentiometer. Check for loose connections within the top housing. Check the rotary switch for burning or other visible damage. Check contact continuity or resistance with a multimeter or short out each speed terminal to verify the switch contacts. If the switch is in good condition one or more speed coils may have failed.

The motor makes excessive noises: Visually check and clean the prop and if it is fouled with weed or damaged get it repaired. Check prop nut and tighten if needed. With the prop off, turn at a medium speed, and check for a bent motor armature. Rotate by hand; if noisy the permanent magnet may be cracked or chipped. When turning it, you should feel what is called magnet drag. Noise and binding may also be caused by worn bearings.

The motor will not switch off: The control micro-switch or the on/off switch may be faulty. Check with a meter and replace. The toggle switch contacts may be burned or welded together.

The foot pedal will not switch motor on: The steering cable may be loose or broken at the foot pedal actuator. Check that the motor has not come loose on the column. Check for any water in the motor. Check for any broken control cables.

ABOUT TRIM TAB TROLLING SYSTEMS

Lenco have an integrated trolling motor and trim tab. These are rated at 164-lb total thrust and for 24 VDC operation. Essentially the same wiring rules apply as for other equipment, requiring a minimum of 6 AWG and a 60-amp Maxi fuse as protection. They come with forward and reverse and two speed operation modes.

ABOUT ELECTRIC OUTBOARD MOTORS

Electric outboards are now becoming more popular for lakes or for inland river navigation. The Outboard Electric Corporation outboards use "Slotless" and brushless DC motors. The conventional DC motor uses brushgear and commutator, which are relatively inefficient at high loads and must dissipate excess heat from the windings. The brushless units have windings outside the permanent magnet segments and dissipate easily through the motor casing to the water. Ray electric outboard have a top mounted electric motor drive unit. Reservoir Runner units also have custom designed permanent magnet motors. Speed control uses a PWM controller. The motors in use produce 4 hp at 48 volts with a current draw of 75 amps. The 6 hp runs on 60 volts and draws 90 amps. In the 72-volt system the controller limits the voltage to 60 volts.

BATTERY VOLTAGES AND SIZES

The size of the battery bank and the voltage depend on the proposed use of the boat. Voltages come in 24-, 36-, 48-, 60- and 70-volt ratings. If you are doing longer distance river navigation a greater battery capacity will be required. The larger the boat the larger the output rating, and electric propulsion uses HP rather than thrust ratings. As the ratings get larger the higher voltages are better. The use of 6-volt deep cycle batteries is recommended.

INSTALLATION NOTES

If you install a 60-volt system, this is no longer low voltage. Most battery cables are rated for lower DC voltages and you must check the insulation ratings for the cables. Some boaters will use welding cables with the higher rated values. The higher the voltage the greater the tracking and leakage risk. You must keep battery tops clean and dry and ensure live parts and terminals are covered.

3

DOWNRIGGERS AND ION SYSTEMS

ABOUT ELECTRIC DOWNRIGGERS

The downrigger has really made an impact, especially in saltwater professional tournaments. Manual units come in powerful electrical versions that allow 12-lb (5-kg) leads. These units often have ion emission systems to attract fish, and automatic bottom tracking connected in with the fish finder. They allow the fisherman to drop a lead close to the bottom along with the favorite bait or lure. The selection of downriggers is based on water depth. The deeper you are fishing, the greater the lead, and this requires larger downriggers. Smaller boats may use portable units and larger ones use electric. Manufacturers of electric downriggers include Penn, Big Jon, Cannon, Walker and Scotty. Due to the reduction in sizes, we are seeing more electric units on smaller boats under the 18–20 ft size. Automatic units allow single hand operation which give fast bait presentation and retrieval.

WHAT ARE THE AUTOMATION FEATURES?

Units such as the Cannon Digitroll IV are fully automatic. Descent and retrieval memories allow programming of up to 5 different rates and depths. Some units have a low voltage warning alarm. Most units also incorporate a Soft-Stop to slow down the weight to prevent cable stress and damage. The Auto-Up function will automatically stop the weight at water level. The Cannon has an integral transducer and bottom tracking mode. This allows bottom contour

following and maintaining the bait at a preset distance above it.
These units also have a cycle function that will automatically jig the
bait up and down. The Cannon and Big Jon are shown below.

CANNON DIGITROLL
Courtesy Cannon

BIG JON
Courtesy Big Jon

HOW MUCH POWER DOES IT USE?

A full-sized electric downrigger must be considered when calculating the boat power system. The motor powers a gear drive; some have belt drives. These have retrieval rates of around 20 ft/min with new ones having a capability of 100 and 200 ft/min. This depends on the weights and maintaining a stable voltage at the motor. If a voltage drop occurs the power also falls. The motors do not run continuously. Retrieval may take several minutes with average consumption up to 3–5Ah of battery capacity. The Walkers tournament model draws around 7 amps with a 10-lb weight attached, and Penn Fathom-Master quotes 6 amps. On start up this can momentarily jump to around 20–25 A. If you get snagged on something it can stall out and take around 30 amps. Cable ratings should be rated for 30 amps with a slow blow fuse or circuit breaker. Typical cable size is 12 or 16 AWG depending on distances from the battery and volt drop.

MAINTAINING ELECTRIC DOWNRIGGERS

Keep the units clean and dry. Operating problems are usually caused by loose switch connections creating high resistances and loss of power.

ABOUT ELECTRIC FISH AND FISHING!

There are electricity producers such as electric eels with up to 600-volt outputs. How they don't electrocute themselves is still being researched. Most fish have inherent electric fields generated by the nervous system. Sharks and rays are renowned for their ability to detect electrical fields and vibrations of their prey. Many other fish such as catfish, trout, sturgeon and salmon have a lateral line on their flanks with electro-receptors, and some have them on their heads. The electro-receptor nerve cells show electrical fields and vibrations which are used to detect concealed prey. The basis of electric fish attraction is the use of various field strengths to attract fish. Research and testing has shown that some fish are attracted by a small positive charge and repelled by a strong positive or negative charge. Salmon can detect voltage variations as low as 0.025V. Fish can also transmit electrical signals similar to sonar, and receive the reflected signal back.

WHAT ARE THE ION SYSTEM PRINCIPLES?

The basic principle of ion attraction systems is the generation and control of a positive charge to target specific fish species. This uses the wire of the electric downrigger. Most manufacturers offer the option. Cabela sell the Black Box. The various species of bony and cartilaginous fish have different responses to voltage variations. Some quoted voltages for use with common sportfishing species are: 0.45V—Halibut; 0.5V—Catfish, Sturgeon; 0.6V—Chinook Salmon; 0.65V—Lake, Rainbow and Brown Trout, Kokanee and Coho Salmon, Striped Bass; 0.75V—Sockeye Salmon, Black Bass. Depending on the field strength and polarity a fish species will either be attracted or will go and hide. The ion control principle is based on the natural and inherent voltage of the boat and equipment, and control of this to achieve a steady and stable voltage level on the downrigger.

WHAT IS A BOAT'S NATURAL VOLTAGE?

Every boat has a natural or inherent voltage level. It is not stable and tends to change based on various environmental factors. The natural voltage is a combination of sources. The first is related to the galvanic action between underwater components. The second is the leakage of electrical currents from poor wiring and connections. The third is the induced or radiated fields from current carrying cables. All electrical equipment has an inherent electrical field. The intensity of that field may vary with the current levels.

HOW TO CHECK THE BOAT'S NATURAL VOLTAGE

To check the boats natural voltage a digital multimeter set on the DC voltage range is required. The Cabela black box system has an integral meter that must be selected to the natural voltage mode. The boat should be taken out, ideally to your normal fishing water depths, as voltages are affected by the salinity level and water temperature. The downrigger should be lowered 5–10 feet. Turn off all electrical circuits as well as the main battery switch. Connect the multimeter negative probe on to the battery negative terminal. Place the positive probe on the downrigger cable. The reading should be in the range 0.7 to 0.8

volts. Turn on main battery switch and systematically turn on each electrical circuit. Record the readings on the multimeter for reference. When all the circuits are switched on, start the engine. A reading of more than 0.05 volt indicates an electrical leakage. This is more common on aluminum boats. If there is no downrigger contact there will be an open circuit so this should be checked. If the readings are low, in the 0.1 to 0.5 volt range, the bonding system may be disconnected or have poor contacts. In many small boats there is no bonding system or sacrificial zinc system. In this case make sure that the main outboard, kicker motor, the aluminum hull and battery negatives are connected. The main zinc connection is usually an aluminum anode on the outboard, and this tends to give lower natural voltage levels of 0.2 to 0.3 volts. The outrigger wire must not be grounding out and should be checked. High readings in the range 0.8 volt and above indicate electrical leakages to the hull, and all connections should be checked. Systematically turn off circuits until the high level disappears. If the main battery switch is turned off and readings change this will verify that the electrical leakage is the cause. The final results should be compared against the ideal voltages of your target species.

WHAT ARE THE EFFECTS ON AN ALUMINUM BOAT?

An aluminum boat actually has an advantage over fiberglass as long as it is properly bonded and equipped with zinc anodes. The metal hull serves as the negative side of the electrolysis circuit and the downrigger wires are the positive side. With the large aluminum hull area, a wide electric field is set up in the water below the boat. With the broader electric zone, fish are attracted from a broader area. All metal hull boats have a large negative "footprint" and can have a fishing advantage. Check the zinc sacrificial anodes on the boat and on your outboard. If they are more than 50% wasted, they should be replaced. If they have a coating of slime or growth, this should be cleaned off. Use a stainless steel brush or a non-metallic scrubber so that the zinc is not contaminated with a foreign material. New zinc anodes should meet MIL-SPEC MIL-18001 (Zinc, -0.1% cadmium and -.025 aluminum).

HOW MUCH POWER DOES AN ION SYSTEM USE?

The ion system has low power consumption, and consumes approximately 0.1 amp. The ion systems have a very small DC output current. They do not or should not create any interference on electronics.

4

TRIM TABS

WHAT DO TRIM TABS DO?

The trim tab allows the running attitude of the boat to be adjusted. The trim control switch supplies a voltage to a pump or actuator to extend (down) or raise (up) the tab. As the tab goes down it deflects water and creates lift. This lift in the stern then forces the bow down.

ABOUT ELECTRIC TRIM TABS

There is the electro-hydraulic and the electric trim tab. The Lectrotab electric type has a reversible DC motor which is torque limited to protect the gearbox and current limited to protect the motor. The actuator has a sealed and greased 40:1 planetary gearbox connected to a high torque drive and ballscrew.

ABOUT ELECTRO-HYDRAULIC TRIM TABS

The electro-hydraulic system has a gear pump. When power is supplied to the pump it turns and the pump pressurizes the system. The solenoid activates to supply pressurized oil through tubing to the piston, ram or actuator cylinder. The rams extend lower or retract to raise the trim tab. Retraction is usually by an internal spring or vacuum. If there are kinks in the tubes this will restrict or prevent fluid flow.

ABOUT AUTOMATIC TRIM TABS

Bennett make an automatic trim system, requiring the use of an attitude transducer. The transducer is connected to a central processing unit (CPU) and an auto trim control (ATC) module. The trim indicator and trim control cables are connected to the ATC modules. The transducer must be installed as low down and level as possible. Any off-zero position is compensated for during zero calibration. Systems require a 20-amp power supply.

HOW MUCH POWER DOES THE TRIM TAB REQUIRE?

For a 12-volt system power consumption is 9 amps to around 20 amps, dependent on the load. If the cables are undersized, a common occurrence, there will be voltage drops and reduced power to operate. The supply cable must be fused.

ABOUT TRIM TAB WIRING COLOR CODES

Positive to switch is orange or red. Motor forward is usually red. Motor reverse is usually yellow. Solenoid port is green (Trim Master and Boat Leveler); red (Bennett); blue (Teleflex). Solenoid starboard is white (Trim Master and Boat Leveler); green (Bennett); yellow (Teleflex). Negative ground is black.

TROUBLESHOOTING TRIM TABS

Nothing happens when switched: Check that the power is on, and that the fuse is not blown. Check the relay operation. Check that all connections are tight at switch and the pump. Make sure ground connection is tight without corrosion.

The pump operates but tabs do not move: Make sure the fluid levels are correct. Check all connections at the switch and pump and that the ground connection is tight without corrosion. Check the pump solenoid connections. Check all tubes for kinks.

Only one tab operates: Make sure all connections are tight at switch and the pump. Make sure ground connection is tight. Check the pump solenoid connections. Reverse the pump hydraulic lines, and see if fault follows. If it swaps there may be some pump blockage.

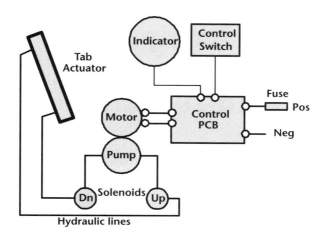

TRIM TAB

5

BATTERIES

WHAT IS THE PURPOSE OF A BOAT BATTERY?

The battery is the power storage device that is used to start the engine or to power lights and accessories, such as radios, pumps and electronics. The battery also acts as a buffer that absorbs the power surges and disturbances during charging and discharging.

WHAT IS THE AMP-HOUR RATING OF A BATTERY?

The Amp-hour rating (Ah) of a battery refers to the available current a battery can deliver over a nominal period until a specified final voltage is reached, or amps per hour. Amp-hour rates are normally specified at the 10- or 20-hour rate. This rating is only applied to deep cycle batteries. For example, a battery is rated at 105 Ah at 10-hour rate, final voltage 1.7 volts per cell. This means that the battery is capable of delivering 10.5 amps for 10 hours, when a cell voltage of 1.7 volts will be reached (Voltage 10.2 Volts).

WHAT IS THE RESERVE CAPACITY RATING OF A BATTERY?

The reserve capacity rating is used to specify the number of minutes a battery can supply a nominal current (25A) at a nominal temperature without the voltage dropping below a nominated level. It indicates the power available when the charging fails and the power available to operate ignition and auxiliaries. Typically, the rating is specified for a 30-minute period at 77°F (25°C) with a final voltage of 10.2 volts.

WHAT IS THE COLD CRANKING AMPS (CCA) RATING?

The cold cranking amp rating specifies the current available at 0°F (-18°C) for a period of 30 seconds, while being able to maintain a cell voltage exceeding 1.2 volts per cell. This is for SAE USA; BS in UK is 60 secs to reach 1.4 volts; EU is 10 secs to reach 1.25 volts. The rating is only applicable for engine starting purposes. The higher the battery rating, the more power available, especially in cold weather conditions.

WHAT IS THE CRANKING AMPS (CA) RATING?

The cranking amp rating is a US rating. It specifies the current available at 32°F (0°C). The Battery Council International requires both CA and CCA to be marked.

WHAT IS THE MARINE CRANKING AMP (MCA) RATING?

The marine cranking amp rating is a relatively new rating which defines the current available at 32°F (0°C) for a period of 30 seconds, while being able to maintain a cell voltage exceeding 1.2 volts per cell. It is similar to CA rating. This rating is only applicable for engine starting purposes. If you are in cold climate area such as the UK, Europe, United States or Canada, the CCA rating is more relevant.

WHAT IS A MARINE BATTERY?

This is a sales or marketing description relating to certain features. The plates may be thicker than normal or there may be more of them. The internal plate supports may absorb vibration. The battery cases may be manufactured with a resilient rubber compound. The cell filling caps may be of an anti-spill design. In general batteries are of a similar design with very little to distinguish between the automotive types except the label. Look at the spec sheets.

WHAT DO THE GROUP NUMBERS MEAN?

These are standard battery sizes used in the US. The following are for 12-volt batteries that are typically used in boats and will vary according to battery type. Large 8D batteries are now easier to handle with Rolls now having removable 2-volt cell based arrangements.

Group	Ah capacity
24	65–75Ah
27	80–90Ah
31	105 Ah
904D	160 Ah
908D	225 Ah
4D	160–200Ah
8D	220–245Ah

WHAT IS A DUAL PURPOSE BATTERY?

A dual purpose battery is a combination of deep cycle and starting battery. It has both a high cranking capacity with good deep cycling ability. It offers a solution for a smaller boat with a single battery used for outboard, electronics and trolling motor. Typical are the Trolling Thunder and the Power-Troll Sportman series AGM batteries.

WHAT TYPE OF BATTERY IS REQUIRED?

The type of battery required depends on the service or power discharge requirements of the boat. The service requirements can be grouped as house power, deep cycle or service loads; the other requirements are starting or high current loads. When the load type is decided the type of battery can be chosen. This may be the lead-acid flooded cell; the gel cell or the AGM type battery. Leading manufacturers with batteries for trolling motor use include Dual Pro, Trolling Thunder, AC Delco, GNB and Minn Kota.

WHY ARE PLATE NUMBERS QUOTED?

Many battery data sheets specify the number of plates. This is defined as the positive and negative plates within a cell. The more plates installed, the greater the plate material surface area. This increases the current during high current rate discharges. The cranking capacity and cold weather performance are improved.

WHAT IS A STARTING OR HIGH CURRENT LOAD?

Starting loads require large current levels for relatively short time periods. Loads in this category also include the anchor windlass, and electric toilets. The starting type battery is normally used for these applications. The battery rating should allow for worst case starting scenarios, such as very cold temperatures. In cold temperatures the battery efficiency is lowered and engine starting requires greater battery power.

HOW TO SELECT START BATTERIES?

The starting battery must be capable of delivering the outboard starter motor with sufficient current to crank over and start the engine. This starting load can be increased by engine compression, oil viscosity and engine driven loads. Loads such as a trolling motor or anchor windlass under full load also require similar high values of current. The starting battery is normally selected on the basis of the engine manufacturers' recommendations. It is good practice to have a safety margin for multi-start capability. Also allow for colder climates where more engine start current is required, as batteries are less efficient when very cold.

HOW A START BATTERY IS CONSTRUCTED

The starting battery contains relatively thin, closely spaced porous plates, which gives maximum exposure of active plate material to the electrolyte with minimal internal resistance. This enables maximum chemical reaction rates, and maximum current availability.

CAN START BATTERIES BE DEEP CYCLED?

Starting batteries cannot withstand cycling, and if deep cycled or flattened, they have an extremely short service life. Ideally they should be maintained within 95% of full charge. Cycle life can be as low as 25–50 cycles. Start batteries, if not fully recharged, will suffer from sulfation. If improperly used for deep cycle applications and undercharged they will sulfate.

WILL START BATTERIES SELF DISCHARGE?

Starting batteries have very low self-discharge rates; this is generally not a problem in normal engine installations.

HOW SHOULD START BATTERIES BE RECHARGED?

The discharged current must be restored quickly to avoid damage, and charge voltages should compensate for temperature. Normally after a high current discharge of relatively short duration, there is no appreciable decrease in electrolyte density. The battery is quickly recharged, as the counter voltage phenomenon does not have time to build up and thus has a negligible effect on the charging.

ABOUT TROLLING MOTOR BATTERIES

A starting type battery is able to supply greater currents, but when the trolling motor is used consistently on a fishing trip, the battery discharges or deep cycles. The starting battery does not last long when deep cycled. The deep cycle battery allows repeated deep discharges without damage. There is a good case for installing 6-volt golf cart type traction batteries. A motor drawing 35 amps at the high speed setting will discharge a 205 Ah deep cycle in 3 hours; running at average of half speed of 18 amps the run time will give at least 6 hours. Time period calculation must be based on your worst case scenario.

WHAT IS A DEEP CYCLE BATTERY?

Service loads require a battery that can withstand cycles of long continuous discharge, and repeated recharging. Suitably named deep cycle batteries are available in all battery types.

WHAT IS A DEEP CYCLE LOAD?

Deep cycle, service or house power loads draw current over long time periods. Equipment includes the cabin lights, refrigeration, electronic instruments, radios, radar, autopilots, inverters, trolling motors and entertainment systems. The deep cycle battery is normally used to supply these applications. Calculations are based on the maximum power consumption over the longest estimated period between battery recharging. Where high current equipment i.e. trolling motor, can cause system disturbances such as large load surges and voltage droops, it is advisable to install a separate battery bank with the required characteristics to power the equipment.

HOW IS THE DEEP CYCLE BATTERY CONSTRUCTED?

The lead acid deep cycle battery is typified by the use of thick, high-density flat-pasted plates, or a combination of flat and tubular. The plate materials may also contain small proportions of antimony to help stiffen them. Porous, insulating separators are used between the plates. Glass matting assists in retaining active material on the plates that may break away as they expand and contract during charge and recharge cycles. If material accumulates at the cell base, a cell short circuit may occur, although this is less common in modern batteries. If material is lost the plates will have reduced capacity or insufficient active material to sustain the chemical reaction with resultant cell failure. Stronger and more efficient plates have been developed; Rolls have their Rezis-tox positive plates. The grid design has fewer heavier sections to hold the high density active material. This is due to the dynamic forces that normally cause expansion and contraction with subsequent warping and cracking. The separator design has also evolved. Rolls use double insulated thick glass woven ones that totally encase the positive plate along with a microporous polyethylene envelope. This retains any material shed from the plates that cause cell short circuiting.

HOW MANY DEEP CYCLES ARE AVAILABLE?

The number of available deep cycles varies between the different makes and models. Typically it is within the range of 800–1500 cycles of discharge to 50% of nominal capacity and then complete recharging. Battery life is a function of the number of cycles and the depth of cycling. Batteries discharged to only 70% of capacity will last much longer than batteries that are discharged to 40% of capacity. Plan your system so that discharge is limited to 50% of battery capacity. The typical life of batteries if they are properly recharged and cycle capabilities maximized can be 5–10 years.

HOW IS A DEEP CYCLE BATTERY SELECTED?

Many boat electrical power problems are caused by improperly selected batteries. Many battery bank capacities are seriously underrated which causes power shortages. If batteries are overrated the charging system cannot properly recharge them, and sulfation of the plates can occur with premature failure. All the electrical equipment on the boat must be listed along with the power consumption ratings.

CONVERTING POWER TO CURRENT

The ratings can be found on the equipment nameplates or in equipment manuals. The ratings are given in amps (A) or watts (W). When watts are used, the rating should be converted to current in amps. To do this, divide the power rating in watts by the operating voltage, 12 or 24 volts.

Power Conversion Table

Watts (W)	Amps (A)
6 watts	0.5 amp
12 watts	1.0 amp
18 watts	1.5 amps
24 watts	2.0 amps
36 watts	3.0 amps
48 watts	4.0 amps
60 watts	5.0 amps
72 watts	6.0 amps

ABOUT BATTERY CAPACITY REQUIREMENTS

The consumption rate on a smaller fishing boat is typically based on a 6-hour period, and a battery bank that is similarly rated at the 10-hour rate is required. In practice you will not match the precise required capacity; therefore you should go to the next battery size up. If you choose a battery that has 240 amp-hours at the 20-hour rate, in effect you will be installing a battery that in the calculated service has 10–15% more capacity than stated on the label.

WHAT IS A LOAD CALCULATION TABLE?

A load calculation table is used to list and carry out calculations. To calculate the total boat electrical system loading, multiply the total current values by the number of operating hours to get the amp-hour rating. If equipment uses a current of 1 amp over an 8-hour period, it consumes 8 Amp-hours (Ah). The table shows many typical power consumptions. There is space for insertion and calculation of your own boat electrical load current data.

WHAT TIME PERIODS SHOULD BE USED?

The calculation period will be based on the total fishing period without use of engine or other charging sources. In most cases the batteries will be charged prior to going in the water, and additional top up may come from the outboard when traveling to the fishing spot. In some cases where several locations are fished, there may also be some additional outboard engine top-up charging. The typical period is 6 to 8 hours and up to 12 with a long fishing vacation or tournament.

HOW SHOULD INTERMITTENT LOADS BE CALCULATED?

On small fishing boats there are few loads that come on and off periodically such as water pumps, using battery power for short periods. It is difficult to quantify actual real current demands with intermittent loads. I use a baseline of 6 minutes per hour, which is 0.1 of an hour. A trolling motor can be classified as an intermittent load. Don't underestimate this. Competition anglers should factor in 100% loads.

HOW TO PERFORM A LOAD CALCULATION

All equipment on the boat must be listed along with the power consumption ratings into a worksheet or table. Ratings are found on the equipment nameplates and in equipment manuals. Insert your own values into the current column, typical values are in brackets. To convert power in watts, to the current in amps, divide the power value by the system voltage. Add up all the current figures relevant to your boat and multiply by hours to determine the average amp-hour consumption rate. Most equipment will be on when drifting and fishing. Depending on the frequency between charging periods select the column that suits your activities.

DC Load Calculation Table

Equipment	Current (A)	Consumption (Ah)
VHF – Receive	(0.5A)	
VHF Transmit	(4.0A)	
GPS	(0.5A)	
Radar	(4.0A)	
Fishfinder LCD	(1.0A)	
Fishfinder Color	(3.0A)	
Instruments	(0.5A)	
Stereo/CD	(1.0A)	
Anchor Light	(1.0A)	
Refrigeration	(4.0A)	
Courtesy Lights	(2.0A)	
Trolling Motor	(35A)	
Livewell Pump	(3.0A)	
Aerator	(2.0A)	
Bilge Pump	(2.0A)	
Downrigger	(8.0A)	
Trim Tabs	(20A)	
UW Camera	(0.5A)	
Pot Puller	(10A)	
TOTAL	**A**	**Ah**

CAN ALL THE BATTERY CAPACITY BE USED?

Nominally it can, but in practice this is rarely possible. For example, if our calculation comes to 10 amps for 6 hours we have a requirement for 60 Ah. For a deep cycle battery the discharge capacity should be kept at 50% of nominal battery capacity to maximize life, so we double the required rating to 120 Ah. This should be a minimum requirement, but certain reality factors must now be introduced into the equation. Factors can vary by 10–30%. Lost capacity is where an older battery no longer has full capacity availability, and the percentage increases with age. In many cases the battery is not fully charged and this also decreases capacity:

Nominal battery capacity		120 Ah
Max cycling level (50%)	Deduct	60 Ah
Lost capacity (10%)	Deduct	12 Ah
Actual charge level (90%)	Deduct 10%	12 Ah
Available Battery Capacity		**36 Ah**

WHAT IS BATTERY LOAD MATCHING?

The nominal required battery capacity of 120 Ah is the required capacity to supply 10 amps per hour over 6 hours to 50% of battery capacity. What is needed is a battery bank with similar discharge rates as the boats electrical current consumption rate. This will maximize the capacity of the battery bank.

WHAT HAPPENS IF THE BATTERY IS DISCHARGED FASTER THAN THE NOMINAL RATE?

The faster a battery is discharged over the nominal rating, either the 10- or 20-hour rate, the less the real amp-hour capacity the battery has. This effect is defined by Peukerts Equation, which has a logarithmic characteristic. This equation is based on the high and low discharge rates and discharge times for each to derive the Peukert coefficient 'n'. Average values are around 1.10 to 1.20. If we discharge a 250 amp-hour battery bank, which has nominal battery discharge rates for each identical battery of 12 amps per hour at a rate of 16 amps, we will actually have approximately 10–15% less capacity. Smart battery discharge meters such as the E-Meter incorporate this coefficient into the monitoring and calculation process.

WHAT HAPPENS WHEN THE BATTERY IS SLOWLY DISCHARGED?

The slower the battery is discharged over the nominal rate the greater the real battery capacity. If we discharge our 240 amp-hour battery bank at 6 amps per hour we will actually have approximately 10–15% more capacity. The disadvantage here is that slowly discharged batteries are harder to charge if deep cycled below 50%.

DOES A DEEP CYCLE SUFFER FROM MEMORY EFFECT?

These batteries do not suffer memory effect and the practice of running them right down and then recharging actually shortens the life of the battery. Keep discharge to a maximum of 50%.

WHAT IS INTERNAL IMPEDANCE OR RESISTANCE?

The battery internal circuit has resistance or impedance. This includes the plates, the electrolyte, internal connections, etc. It affects both the rate of discharge and rate of charge. The lower the impedance the greater the charge and discharge rates and the less heat generated and power lost.

HOW DOES A FLOODED CELL LEAD ACID BATTERY WORK?

When two electrodes of different metal are placed in an electrolyte, they form a galvanic cell. An electrochemical process then takes place within each cell which generates a voltage. In the typical flooded lead-acid cell the generated voltage is nominally 2.1 volts per cell. In a normal flooded cell lead-acid battery, water loss will occur when it is electrically broken down into oxygen and hydrogen near the end of charging. In normal batteries, the gases disperse to atmosphere, resulting in electrolyte loss. These are the bubbles seen in the cells during charging.

WHAT ARE THE COMPONENTS OF A BATTERY CELL?

The typical 12-volt battery consists of 6 cells, which are internally connected in series to make up the battery. The battery cell is made up of several basic components.

- Lead dioxide (PbO_2), the positive plate active material, brown in color.
- Lead peroxide (Pb), the negative plate material, grey in color.
- Sulfuric acid (H_2SO_4), the electrolyte in a diluted solution with water.
- The grids, which hold the lead dioxide and lead peroxide plate material. Antimony is used along with calcium on newer batteries, which improves performance and battery life.
- The separators, which hold or space the plates apart.
- The battery casing, used to contain each cell.
- The terminals, used to connect the cells.

WHAT IS AN ELECTROLYTE AND SPECIFIC GRAVITY?

The proper term for the battery acid is electrolyte, a dilute solution of sulfuric acid and water. Specific gravity (SG) is the measurement used to define electrolyte acid concentration. A fully charged battery cell has an SG typically in the range 1.240 to 1.280, corrected for temperature. This is an approximate volume ratio of acid to water of 1:3. Pure sulfuric acid has an SG of 1.835, and water has a nominal 1.0. The SG of a battery is an indicator of battery charge level.

ABOUT SPECIFIC GRAVITY INDICATORS

Many batteries such as the AC Delco-Voyager batteries have a small clear indicator window. The internal eye changes color to indicate charge status. Green indicates approximately 75% charge level, dark indicates 50–75% charge level, and red indicates less than 50% charge level.

WHAT HAPPENS WHEN A CELL DISCHARGES?

When an external load such as a light is connected across the positive and negative terminals, the cell will discharge. As there is a potential or voltage difference between the two poles, electrons will flow from the negative pole to the positive pole. A chemical reaction then takes place between the two plate materials and the electrolyte. During the discharge reaction, the plates interact with the electrolyte to form lead sulfate and water. This reaction dilutes the electrolyte, reducing the density. As both the plates become similar in composition, the cell loses the ability to generate a voltage.

HOW IS A CELL RECHARGED?

The charging process reverses the discharge reaction. The water decomposes to release the hydrogen and oxygen. The two plate materials are then restored to the original material. When the plates are fully restored and the electrolyte is returned to the nominal density. the battery is completely recharged.

HOW DOES TEMPERATURE AFFECT THE READINGS?

For accuracy, all hydrometer readings should be corrected for temperature. Actual cell temperatures should be used, but ambient battery temperatures are sufficient. Hydrometer floats usually have the reference temperature printed on them and this should be used for calculations. For every 2.7°F (1.5°C) the cell temperature is *above* the reference value *add* 1 point (0.001) to the hydrometer reading. For every 2.7°F (1.5°C) the cell temperature is *below* the reference value *subtract* 1 point (0.001) from the hydrometer reading. For example if the reference temperature is 68°F (20°C), at a temperature of 77°F (25°C), add 0.004 to the reading. If the temperature is near freezing at 41°F (5°C), deduct 0.012 from the reading.

HOW IMPORTANT IS BATTERY WATER?

When topping up the cell electrolyte, always use distilled or de-ionized water. Rainwater is acceptable, but never use water out of the galley tap or faucet, as this generally has an excessive mineral content or other impurities that pollute and damage the cells. Impurities introduced into the cell will remain, and concentrations will accumulate at each top up reducing service life.

WHAT IS PLATE SULFATION?

Plate sulfation is the most common cause of battery failure. When a battery is discharged the chemical reaction converts both plates to lead sulfate. If recharging is not carried out quickly, the lead sulfate starts to harden and crystallize. This is shown by white crystals on the brown plates and is almost non-reversible. The immediate effect of sulfation is partial and permanent loss of capacity as the active plate materials are reduced. Electrolyte density also partially decreases, as the chemical reaction during charging cannot be fully reversed. This sulfated material introduces higher resistances within the cell and inhibits charging. As the level of sulfated material increases, the cell loses the capability to retain a charge and the battery fails.

HOW EFFICIENT IS A BATTERY?

Battery efficiency is affected by temperature. At 32°F (0°C), the efficiency will fall by 60%. Batteries in warm tropical climates are more efficient, but may have reduced life spans, and batteries commissioned in tropical areas often have lower acid densities. Batteries in cold climates have increased operating lives, but are less efficient.

WHAT IS SELF DISCHARGE?

During charging, small particles of the antimony used in the plates, and other impurities dissolve out of the positive plates and deposit on to the negative ones. Other impurities from impure topping up water also deposit on the plates. A localized chemical reaction then takes place, slowly discharging the cell. Self-discharge rates are affected by temperature. At 32°F (0°C), the self-discharge rates are small. At 86°F (30°C), the self-discharge rates are very high and the specific gravity can decrease by as much as 0.002 per day, typically up to 4% per month.

WHEN SHOULD A BATTERY BE RECHARGED?

A deep cycle battery should be recharged when the charge level falls to a maximum of 50%. A starting battery should always be recharged immediately after each use. If a start battery is deep cycled the life of the battery will be severely reduced. As soon as the boat gets home the batteries should be charged; don't even leave it overnight as it causes damage.

WHAT HAPPENS WHEN A BATTERY
IS COMPLETELY DISCHARGED?

Deep cycle batteries are permanently damaged by sulfation of plates. Gel batteries can survive up to a month, while AGMs can survive also about a month. All can be recharged; however damage occurs and cycle life is reduced.

HOW HAZARDOUS ARE BATTERIES?

The lead-acid battery cells contain an explosive mixture of hydrogen and oxygen gas at all times. An explosion risk exists if naked flames, sparks or cigarettes are introduced into the immediate vicinity. Always use insulated tools. Cover the terminals with an insulating material to prevent accidental short circuit and sparks. Watchbands, bracelets and neck chains can accidentally cause a short circuit. Sulfuric acid is highly corrosive and must be handled with extreme caution. Always lift the battery with carriers if fitted. If no carriers are fitted, lift using opposite corners to prevent case distortion and electrolyte spills. Always connect the positive cable first and negative last. Disconnect the negative first and positive last.

ABOUT CONNECTING THE BATTERIES

When connecting batteries, quality battery terminals must be used. The type with wing nuts should not be used as they are hard to tension up without breaking the ears or wings off. Always use a bolt type or clamp type connector. The clamp type does not require a terminal lug. It is also good protection to install a terminal cover over the connection to prevent accidental contact.

WHERE SHOULD BATTERIES BE INSTALLED?

Batteries should be installed as close as practicable to the system or equipment they power. This becomes a real problem when installing trolling motor batteries, as bow mount units require a lot of weight when installed forward. Installing them aft requires a long run of heavy duty cables. The batteries should never be installed close to any source of ignition, such as the fuel tanks and system parts such as fuel filters, separators and valves. Batteries should be contained within PVC battery boxes located at the opposite side of the boat to any fuel systems. Battery boxes must be fastened down and tie down straps are available. Insert rubber spacers around the batteries to stop any movements and vibrations. In small boats the weight of a battery can cause a lot of movement when planing and slamming across wave tops. Battery box lids should be in place at all times and secured. PVC or other connection covers should be installed where accidental contact by tools or other items can cause a short circuit across the terminals. A short circuited battery can generate currents exceeding 5,000 amps!

WHEN ARE BATTERIES CONNECTED IN SERIES?

Batteries are connected in series to increase the voltage. Batteries and cells with ratings of 1.2V, 6V and 12V can be connected in series to make up banks of 12V, 24V, 32V, 36V or 48V. Six-volt batteries are frequently used in 12 and 24 volt systems as they are easier to install and remove. When connecting batteries in series the batteries should be of the same rating, model and age. If one battery requires replacement the other should also be replaced. In some installations a series-parallel switch or relay is used to connect batteries for 24 or 36 volts to power trolling motors.

WHEN ARE BATTERIES CONNECTED IN PARALLEL?

Batteries are connected in parallel to increase the rating or amp/hour power capacity for the same voltage. Batteries up to around 115Ah can be easily handled with parallel banks of up to three being a common arrangement.

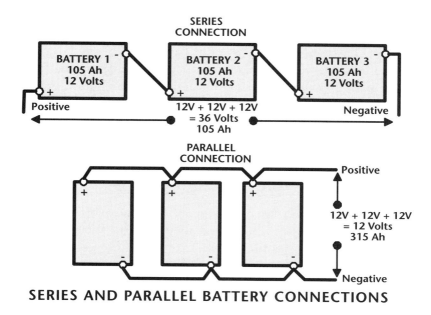

SERIES AND PARALLEL BATTERY CONNECTIONS

HOW ARE BATTERY NEGATIVES CONNECTED?

When two or more batteries are connected in parallel all the battery negatives are also connected together. When a house battery bank and a starting battery are charged from the same source the negatives are also connected. The polarizing ground is then connected to one of the battery negatives. In dual battery systems the cables connecting each battery negative or positive should be rated the same.

WHAT BATTERY MAINTENANCE IS REQUIRED?

Check the density of the electrolyte but do not test immediately after charging or discharging. Wait at least half an hour until the cells stabilize, as it takes some time for the pockets of varying electrolyte densities to equalize. Never test immediately after topping up the electrolyte. Wait until after a charging period, as it takes time for the water to mix evenly. Check the electrolyte level in each cell. Always top up electrolyte levels with de-ionized or distilled water to the correct levels. Clean the battery surfaces with a clean, damp cloth.

Moisture, salt and other surface contaminations can cause surface leakage between the positive and negative terminals across the battery casing top. This can slowly discharge the battery and is a common cause of dead batteries, and mysterious but untraceable system leaks. Clean the terminals up along with any verdigris using a solution of baking soda and water. Ensure that the terminal posts are clean and tight, then apply a coating of Vaseline. When the boat is not in use it is better to disconnect and remove the battery from the boat.

WHAT IS A LOAD TEST?

A fully charged battery has a load connected along with a digital voltmeter. Typically the load is rated at about half the rated CCA value and is often around 300 amps. This is connected for 15 seconds. The voltage at the end of this period is an indicator of condition and the capability to sustain the electrical chemical reaction. A reading over 9.6 volts indicates that the battery is still serviceable; a lower reading indicates that the battery is failing. It is both easy and inexpensive (often at no cost) to get your local auto electrician to do a load test.

WHAT ARE ABSORBED GLASS MAT (AGM) OR VALVE REGULATED LEAD ACID (VRLA) BATTERIES?

These are new generation battery types. The electrolyte is held within a very fine microporous, boron-silicate glass matting that is placed between the plates. This absorbs and immobilizes the acid while still allowing plate interaction. The batteries are also called starved electrolyte batteries, as the mat is only 95% soaked in electrolyte.

HOW DOES AN AGM BATTERY WORK?

These batteries use a principle called recombinant gas absorption. The plates and separators are held under pressure. During charging, the evolved oxygen is only able to move through the separator pores from positive to negative, reacting with the lead plate. The negative plate charge is effectively maintained below 90%, which stops hydrogen generation.

HOW ARE AGM BATTERIES CHARGED?

Typical charge voltages are in the range 14.4 to 14.6 volts at 68°F (20°C). The batteries have a very low internal resistance, resulting in minimal heating effects during heavy charge and discharge. They can be bulk charged at very high currents, typically by a factor of five over flooded cells, and a factor of 10 over gel batteries. They also allow 30% deeper discharges and recharge 20% faster than gel batteries, and have good recovery from full discharge conditions. Self-discharge rates are only 1%–3%. At high temperatures both AGM and gel cells are unable to dissipate the heat generated by oxygen and hydrogen recombination and this can create thermal runaway. This will lead to gassing and the drying out of cells. A premature loss of capacity can occur when the positive plate and grids degrade with higher operating temperatures due to the recombination process and higher charge currents.

WHAT IS A GEL BATTERY?

The gel cell has a solidified gel as an electrolyte, which is locked into each group of plates. During charging the gel liquefies due to its thixotropic properties, and solidification after charging can exceed an hour as thixotropic gels have a reduced viscosity under stress. The newer battery types use phosphoric acid in the gel to retard the sulfation hardening rates.

HOW IS A GEL BATTERY CONSTRUCTED?

The lead plates in a gel cell are reinforced with calcium, rather than the antimony used in flooded cells. This reduces self-discharge rates, and they are relatively thin. This also helps gel diffusion and improves the charge acceptance rate as diffusion problems are reduced. The separator provides electrical and mechanical isolation of the plates. Each cell has a safety valve to relieve the excess pressure if the set internal pressure is exceeded. The valve will then re-close tightly to prevent oxygen from entering the cell.

HOW ARE GEL BATTERIES CHARGED?

The gel battery has a higher charge acceptance rate than the flooded cell battery. This allows a more rapid charge rate; the typical rate is 50% of Ah capacity. A gel cell battery cannot tolerate having any equalizing charge applied and this over charge condition will seriously damage them. During charging the current causes decomposition of the water and the generation of oxygen at the positive plate. The oxygen diffuses through the unfilled glass mat separator pores to the negative plate, and chemically reacts to form lead oxide, lead sulfate and water. The charge current then reduces and does not evolve hydrogen gas. If recombination of hydrogen is incomplete during overcharge conditions, the gases may vent to the battery locker. While these batteries will accept some 30–40% greater current than an equivalent lead acid battery, they are restricted in the voltage levels allowed, so you cannot use any fast charging system. The normal optimum voltage tolerance on Dryfit units is 14.4 volts. There are some minimal heating effects during charging, caused by the recombination reaction. Continuous over or undercharging of gel cells is the most common cause of premature failure. In many cases this is due to use of automotive type chargers.

ADVANTAGES AND DISADVANTAGES
OF BATTERY TYPES

Advantages:

Flooded or Wet Cell Batteries. They cost less, are lighter in weight, and more resilient to overcharge conditions.

Gel Cell Batteries. They don't require maintenance, don't spill acid or generate gas in normal operation. They also have low self discharge rates, and some have good deep cycle ability.

AGM Batteries. They don't require maintenance, and don't spill acid or generate gas in normal operation. They have high charge acceptance rates, and a low self discharge rates, good deep cycle ability and maintain a relatively constant voltage during discharge.

Disadvantages:

Flooded or Wet Cell Batteries. Maintenance is required, acid can be spilled, gases are generated, and they have relatively high self-discharge rates.

Gel Cell Batteries. They are expensive, heavier, and if they suffer overcharging they are permanently damaged.

AGM Batteries. They are expensive, heavy, and if they suffer overcharging they are permanently damaged.

Average State of Charge – Voltage

State	Flooded	Gel	AGM
100%	12.75V	12.90V	12.85V
75%	12.40V	12.65V	12.60V
50%	12.25V	12.35V	12.30V
25%	12.00V	12.00V	12.00V
0%	11.65V	11.80V	11.80V

CAN THE BATTERY TYPES BE MIXED?

Battery types must not be mixed. Each battery type has a different charging voltage and discharge characteristic, so the battery types must be the same. Also never mix old batteries with new batteries.

WHAT IS THE LIFE EXPECTANCY OF EACH BATTERY TYPE?

Numbers are usually based on the manufacturers' data. A quality deep cycle lead acid traction battery can have a life exceeding 2500 cycles of charge and discharge to 50%. A gel cell can have a life of approximately 500–800 cycles depending on the make. An AGM battery has a cycle life of 350 to 2200 depending on the type.

6

BATTERY CHARGING

ABOUT CHARGING EFFICIENCY

Manufacturers specify nominal capacities of batteries, and the total capacity of the bank must be taken into consideration. Older batteries have reduced capacities due to normal in-service aging, and plate sulfation, which increases internal resistance and also inhibits the charging process. The electrolyte is temperature dependent, and the temperature is a factor in setting maximum charging voltages. The state of charge at charging commencement can be checked using the open circuit voltage test and electrolyte density. The level of charge will affect the charging rate.

WHAT IS THE CORRECT CHARGING VOLTAGE?

Charging voltage is defined as the battery voltage plus the cell voltage drops. Cell volt drops are due to internal resistance, plate sulfation, electrolyte impurities and gas bubble formation that occur on the plates during charging. These resistances oppose the charging and must be exceeded to effectively recharge the battery. Resistance to charging increases as a fully charged state is reached and decreases with discharge. A battery is self-regulating in terms of the current it can accept when being charged. Over-current charging at excessive voltages simply generates heat and damages the plates.

Volts	Fast Charge Average	Float Average
12 V	14.5 V	13.6 V
24 V	29.0 V	27.2 V
36 V	43.5 V	40.8 V

WHAT DOES BULK CHARGE MEAN?

The bulk charge phase is the initial charging period where charging takes place until the gassing point is reached. This is typically in the range 14.4 to 14.6 volts corrected for temperature, and this is also termed current limited charging. The bulk charge rate can be anywhere between 25% and 40% of rated amp-hour capacity at the 20-hour rate as long as temperature rises are limited.

WHAT DOES ABSORPTION CHARGE MEAN?

After attaining the gassing voltage, the charge level should be maintained at 14.4 volts until the charge current falls to 5% of battery capacity. This is termed voltage limited charging. This level is normally 85% of capacity. In a typical 300 amp-hour bank, this is 15 amps.

WHAT IS A FLOAT CHARGE?

The battery charge rate should be reduced to a float voltage of approximately 13.2 to 13.8 volts to maintain the battery at full charge.

WHAT IS AN EQUALIZATION CHARGE?

An equalization charge is the application of a higher voltage level at a current rate of 5% of battery capacity. This is done to "re-activate" the plates. It will not completely reverse the effects of sulfation. There may be an improvement following the process, but it will not reverse long-term permanent damage. Equalization at regular intervals can increase battery longevity by ensuring complete chemical conversion of plates, but care must be taken. Equalization charges are typically set at 16.5

volts for up to 3 hours so it is essential that all circuits be off at the switch panel so that higher voltages cannot damage equipment power supplies.

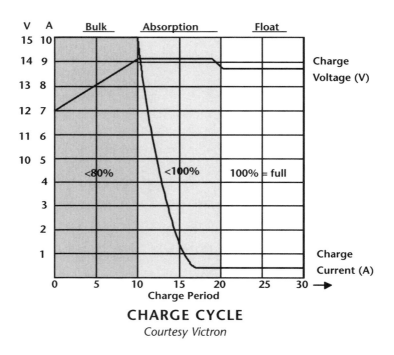

CHARGE CYCLE
Courtesy Victron

WHAT IS THE CORRECT CHARGING CAPACITY?

From the power calculation table we have calculated the maximum current consumption. We must add to this a 20% margin for battery losses to give a final charging value. A battery requires the replacement of 120% of the discharged current to restore it to full charge. This value is required to overcome losses within the battery due to battery internal resistances during charging. The charging source rating should be approximately 30 to 40% of the battery capacity. As a battery is effectively self-limiting in terms of charge acceptance levels, it is not possible to simply apply the discharged value and expect the battery to recharge. The battery during charging is reversing the chemical reaction of discharge, and this can only occur at a finite rate. The battery charger must be selected if possible to recharge at the battery optimum charge rate as specified. Charging has a tapered characteristic, which is why start and finishing rates are specified. Newer batteries such as Odyssey or Trolling Thunder AGM types have a very high charge acceptance rate. This is a good characteristic for trolling motors as 80% of a discharged battery current can be restored in an hour. This assumes you have a charging source rated that large.

Typical Battery Charge Levels

Temp	Flooded Hi/Float	Gel Hi/Float	AGM Hi/Float
90°F (32°C)	14/13.1	14.0/13.6	14.4/13.8
80°F (27°C)	14.3/13.3	14.0/13.7	14.5/14.0
70°F (20°C)	14.4/13.5	14.1/13.8	14.6/14.1
60°F (15°C)	14.6/13.7	14.3/13.9	14.7/14.2
50°F (10°C)	14.8/13.9	14.2/14.0	14.8/14.3

WHAT IS COUNTER VOLTAGE (SURFACE CHARGE)?

During charging a phenomenon called counter voltage occurs. This is caused by the inability of the electrolyte in the battery cells to percolate at a sufficiently high rate into the plate material pores and subsequently convert both plate material and electrolyte. This causes the plate surface voltage to rise. The battery will resist charging and "trick" the battery charger or alternator voltage regulator by indicating an artificially high voltage with the recognizable premature reduction in charging. It is often referred to as a "surface charge."

THE DUAL POSITION CHANGEOVER SWITCH

The charging system on most engines uses the same cabling as the engine starter circuit. In two-battery systems this consists of a switch with three positions (1, 1+2, 2 and off). The center position parallels both battery banks. It is not rare to see both batteries left accidentally in parallel under load with the flattening of both. Many are quite un-reliable and are subject to high resistances on contact with large volt drops under high load conditions which often cause starting and charging problems. If a changeover switch is operated under load, the surge will probably destroy the alternator rectifier diodes.

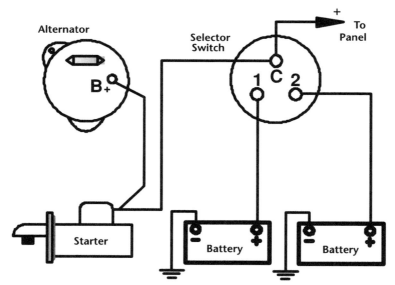

SINGLE ENGINE SWITCH CHARGING CONFIGURATION

WHAT IS THE RELAY OR SOLENOID CONFIGURATION?

This system enables separation of the charging system from starting circuits. The relay or solenoid offers a point of failure if incorrectly rated for the job. The relay connects both batteries during charging, and separates them when off, preventing discharge between the bat-teries. The relay-operating coil is interlocked with the ignition and en-ergizes when the key is turned on. Relay ratings should at least match the maximum rated output of the alternator.

HOW DOES A DIODE ISOLATOR CHARGING SYSTEM WORK?

A diode is a semiconductor one-way valve, consisting of an anode and cathode. It allows electrons to flow one way only and has a high resistance the other way. A diode isolator consists of two diodes with their inputs connected. They allow voltage to pass one way only, so that each battery has an output. This prevents any back feeding between the batteries. They are mounted on heat sinks specifically designed for the maximum current carrying capacity and maximum heat dissipation. They are not commonly used on small fishing boats as the alternators on outboards are not battery sensed and cannot compensate for the voltage drop across the diodes. A diode has an inherent voltage drop of typically 0.7 to 0.8 volt. This is unacceptable in a normal charging circuit.

WHAT ARE SMART BATTERY SWITCHES?

Smart electronic battery switches are a good solution for charging more than one battery bank on fishing boats. They can be used either from charging off outboard engines or from battery chargers when the boat is ashore. These are also known as charge distributors or integrators, or combiners such as the NewMar Battery Bank Integrator (BBI). When a charge voltage is detected that exceeds 13.3 VDC the unit switches on. The unit consists of a low contact resistance relay that closes to parallel the batteries for charging. When charging ceases and voltage falls to 12.7 VDC, the relay opens isolating the batteries. Other devices include the PathMaker which allow charging of two or three batteries from one alternator or battery charger; the Isolator Eliminator from Ample Power, a multi-step regulator that controls charge to the second battery bank, typically used for engine starting. It is temperature compensated like an alternator control system and is effectively a secondary charger. The Battery Mate from Mastervolt is a charge splitter that can supply three batteries, without voltage drop. Another system is the AutoSwitch from Ample Power, a smart solenoid system. An electronic sensing circuit will enable the setting of the different modes. The Hell Roarer is another system as is the DualPro ProXtra II common on bass boats. These reduce the chances of overcharging secondary batteries such as the start or trolling motor battery.

Courtesy Mastervolt   Courtesy Newmar   Courtesy DualPro

CHARGE ISOLATORS AND SPLITTERS

HOW DO BATTERY CHARGERS WORK?

Many small boats have a permanently installed battery charger. This can be charged straight off a portable electric generator or hooked up when the boat is on the trailer at home. Many boat batteries have had the batteries ruined by poor quality chargers due to a marginal over-charge voltage level. The AC mains voltage, either 230 or 110 volts AC is applied to a transformer. The transformer steps down the volt-age to a low level, typically around 15/30 volts depending on the out-put level. A full wave bridge rectifier similar to that in an alternator rectifies the low level AC voltage. The rectifier outputs a voltage of around 13.8/27.6 volts, which is a typical float voltage level. Many basic chargers do not have any output regulation. Chargers that do have regulation are normally those that use systems to control output voltage levels. The sensing circuits automatically limit charge voltages to nominal levels and reduce to float values when the predetermined full charge condition is reached.

WHAT IS A CONSTANT VOLTAGE CHARGER?

It may also be called constant voltage or potential charger and it op-erates at a fixed output voltage, typically 13.4–13.8 volts. Auto charg-ers using a silicon controlled rectifier (SCR) or thyristor are typical. The initial high charge current decreases as the battery terminal volt-age reaches the preset charging voltage. Batteries can sustain damage if unsupervised as electrolytes evaporate, and gas formation can be excessive. Additionally such chargers are susceptible to mains input voltage variations. If left unattended, the voltage setting must be below 13.5 volts, or batteries will be ruined through overcharging.

WHAT IS A FERRO-RESONANT CHARGER?

These chargers use a ferro-resonant transformer, which have two secondary windings. One of the windings is connected to a capacitor, and resonate at a specific frequency. Variations in the input voltage cause an imbalance, and the transformer corrects this to maintain a stable output. These chargers have a tapered charge characteristic. As the battery terminal voltage rises, the charge current decreases. Control of these chargers is usually through a sensing circuit that switches the charger off when the nominal voltage level is reached, typically around 15% to 20% of charger nominal rating. These chargers are not recommended for gel and AGM batteries as they are known to heat and dry them out.

WHAT IS A SWITCH-MODE CHARGER?

Compact switch-mode chargers are becoming increasingly popular due to their compact size and very low weights. These charger types convert the input line frequency from 50 to a high frequency of 150,000 hertz, which reduces the size of transformers and chokes used in conventional chargers. An advantage of these chargers is that line input and output are effectively isolated eliminating the effects of surges and spikes. These chargers are my personal favorites. They are battery sensed, temperature compensated, have integral digital voltmeter and ammeter, and are physically very compact. They also are smart types with selectable charge modes including bulk, acceptance, float and selectable voltages to suit gel, AGM or flooded cell batteries.

ABOUT PULSED CURRENT CHARGERS

These are often called maintainers or conditioning systems rather than chargers. They use a pulsed or high frequency DC output. They are very effective at reversing some of the effects of plate sulfation. They may be useful but do not replace quality higher output chargers.

OFF-VEHICLE CHARGING SYSTEMS

A system called the Stay-N-Charge is based on charging the batteries from the vehicle charging system. This allows you to charge the batteries on the way home or to another site. If camping out without AC, you can charge the batteries by simple running of the vehicle engine. As alternators don't give full output at idle, the engine speed will have to be higher. It is also possible to connect the car battery with jumper leads to the boat batteries.

INSTALLING BATTERY CHARGERS

Chargers should be mounted in a dry location. Do not operate a large load such as the trolling motor with a charger still operating. The large start load can overload the charger and may cause damage to circuits. Proper bolt on terminal lugs should be used on cables if the charger is permanently installed, not clips. Switch off the charger before connecting or disconnecting cables from battery, as sparks may ignite gases. It is important to verify they are ignition protected if installed close to fuel systems.

HOW ARE MULTIPLE BATTERY BANKS CHARGED?

Many boats have a multiple output charger connected permanently. The isolated outputs can charge the start, house and the trolling motor battery banks. Remember that gel cells or AGM batteries may have different requirements and this should be checked prior to using any system. In a 24- or 36-volt trolling battery set up, each output is connected to each of the series connected batteries.

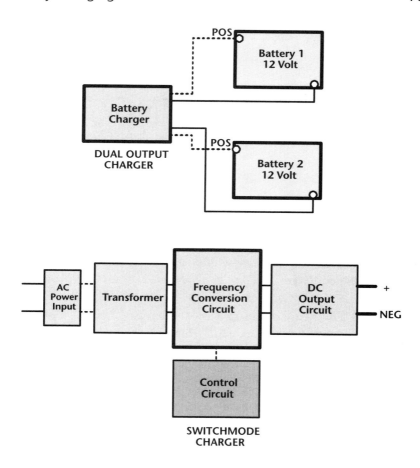

SWITCHMODE
CHARGER

MULTIPLE OUTPUT CHARGERS
Courtesy ChargePro and DualPro

7

BOAT WIRING

WHAT ELECTRICAL STANDARDS ARE REQUIRED?

Small boat electrical systems should be installed as far as practicable to comply with one of the principal standards or recommendations in use. Most standards are similar. They include: **American Boat and Yacht Council (ABYC).** Standards and Recommended Practices for Small Craft; **The United States Coast Guard.** Title 33, CFR 183 Subpart I, Section 183; **European Recreational Craft Directive (UK and Europe).** EN ISO 10133. Small Craft—Electrical systems—Extra-low-voltage d.c. installations, 1994; EN 28846:1993 Electrical devices—Protection against ignition of surrounding flammable gas; EN28849:1993 Electrically operated bilge pumps.

WHICH VOLTAGE SHOULD BE USED?

Most fishing boats have a primary 12-volt system and a 24- or 36-volt system for the trolling motor. The 12-volt system is the most common system. This is because of automotive influences and outboard engines being made with 12-volt systems. The charge voltage is typically 14 volts. For 24-volt systems the charge voltage required is 28 volts. Where two voltages are used they should be treated as two entirely separate systems. In polarized ground systems the negatives will be connected to maintain the same potential. Because much equipment is commonly 12 volts a DC-DC converter must be used to step down to 12-volts. The alternative is to tap off the 12-volt supply from one of the series connected batteries. The advantage of using a DC-DC converter is to isolate sensitive electronics equipment from the surge and spike-prone power system. Where 36 volts is used, three 12-volt battery banks are connected in series to make 36 volts.

USING DC/DC VOLTAGE CONVERTERS

It is common to tap off 12 volts or 24 volts from part of the trolling motor battery bank. A better option is to use a DC to DC voltage converter across the whole battery bank. This will then step down to the required voltage. The quality DC to DC converters will effectively isolate the power supply and filter out any voltage spikes, surges and interference. These are impressed on the battery bank from the trolling motor.

THE TWO-WIRE ONE-POLE GROUNDED WIRING SYSTEM

The two-wire one-pole grounded system is called a polarized system and is the most common configuration. It holds the negative at ground potential by connecting the battery negative to ground, or in most cases the mass of the engine. The main negative to the engine polarizes the system, as the engine mass, an aluminum hull and connected parts provide the ground plane. This is used to polarize the DC electrical system and doesn't actually carry current. In a two-wire, one-pole grounded system, each outgoing circuit positive supply circuit requires a short circuit protection and isolation device installed. This may be incorporated within a single trip free circuit breaker. The earthed pole should not have any protective device installed. In this configuration, a short circuit between positive and ground will cause maximum short circuit current. A short circuit between negative and ground will have no effect. A short between positive and negative will cause maximum short circuit current to flow. The single pole circuit breaker will break positive polarity only.

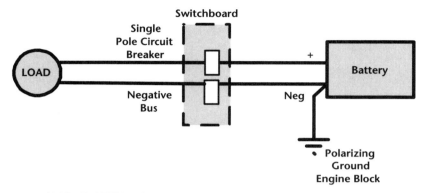

INSULATED ONE-POLE GROUNDED SYSTEMS

HOW ARE WIRE SIZES CALCULATED?

Wire sizes must be selected based on the maximum current demand or ampacity of the circuit. All wires have a nominal cross-sectional area (CSA) and current carrying capacity. Standards specify nominal capacities for a range of cross-sectional areas and temperature ranges.

Typical DC Cable Nominal Current Ratings

AWG	CM Circ Mil	CSA	Area Mm²	DC Amps
20	1024	0.52	0.5	1.5-2
18	1624	0.82	0.75	2-3
17	2052	1.04	1	3-4
16	2581	1.31		
15	3260	1.65	1.5	4.5-6
14	4109	2.08		
13	5184	2.63	2.5	7.5-10

12	6529	3.31		
11	8226	4.17	4	12-16
10	10384	5.26		
9	13087	6.63	6	18-24
8	16512	8.37		
7	20822	10.55	10	30-40
6	26244	13.30		
5	33088	16.77	16	48-64
4	41738	21.15		
3	52624	26.66	25	75-100
2	66358	33.62	35	105-140
1	83694	42.41		
0	105625	53.52	50	150-200
2/0	133079	67.43	70	210-280
3/0	167772	85.01		
4/0	211600	107.21	95	285-380

HOW TO CALCULATE CABLE AND WIRE SIZES

In the US the more common method of calculating cable current ratings, voltage drop and ampacity is the use of charts and tables. The charts are used either for 3% voltage drop for navigation lights, main power feeds and electronics, and 10% for other circuits (See table in Chapter 2). The vertical scale has the current in amps and the horizontal scale is the total length of the circuit. In DC circuits both the positive circuit wire to the equipment and the negative must be added to get the total length. The following formula can be used.

CM = K x I x L/E

CM = Circular Mil area of the conductors

K = 10.75 (a copper resistance constant per mil-foot)

I = Current in amps

L = Conductor length in feet

E = Voltage drop at the load in volts

Example 1: To find CM cable size for 3% voltage drop in a trolling motor circuit with 35-amp motor, conductor distance is 16 feet to a forward mounted unit. Nominal voltage 12.5 volts on charged battery.

CM = K x I x L/E

CM = 10.75 x 35 x 32/.375

CM = 32105 in table, closest is 5 AWG

Example 2: To find voltage drop in a trolling motor circuit with 35-amp motor, conductor supply length is 32 feet to motor using 4 AWG wire.

E = K x I x L/CM

E = 10.75 x 35 x 32/ 41738

Volt drop = .288 volts, 2.3% which is acceptable.

If calculated using 8 AWG

E = 10.75 x 35 x 32/ 16512

Volt Drop = .7292 volts, 5.8% which is unacceptable.

Total circuit resistance R will be the sum of R1 + R2 + R3 + R4 etc.

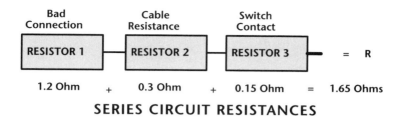

SERIES CIRCUIT RESISTANCES

HOW TO CALCULATE VOLTAGE DROP

Voltage drop is always a consideration when installing electrical circuits. Unfortunately, many voltage drop problems are created by the practice of trying to install the smallest cables and wiring sizes possible. The ABYC sets a recommendation of 3% and 10% for circuits. I recommend having a maximum acceptable voltage drop in 12-volt systems of 5% for all circuits, and aim for 3% on the ABYC required equipment such as navigation lights and electronics. A 10% limit is really excessive for most equipment, in particular circuits such as bilge pumps. The voltage drop problem is prevalent in starting and charging systems, thrusters, windlasses and trolling motors and I recommend 3% maximum. The formula is specified in ISO Standard 10133, Annex A.2.

$$\text{Voltage Drop at Load (volts)} = \frac{0.0164 \times I \times L}{S}$$

I = load current in amperes

L = cable length in meters, positive to load and back to negative.

S = conductor cross-sectional area, in square millimeters

Examples: For a trolling motor these cable sizes must be calculated at normal working load. As the calculations show, a larger cable size ensures less voltage drop and fewer line losses. Full load current = 35, cable run = 32 feet (10m), nominal voltage is 12.5 volts.

$$3 \text{ AWG (25mm) drop at 35 amps} \quad = \quad \frac{0.0164 \times 35 \times 10}{25}$$

$$= \quad 0.2296 \text{ Volts } (1.84\%)$$

$$7 \text{ AWG (10mm) drop at 35 amps} \quad = \quad \frac{0.0164 \times 35 \times 10}{10}$$

$$= \quad 0.574 \text{ Volts } (4.6\%)$$

SELECTING CABLE TYPES

In most small fishing boats single insulated wires are used. When possible, use double insulated cables to ensure insulation integrity. Insulation is temperature rated and in most boats PVC insulated and PVC sheathed cables rated at 170ºF (75ºC) are used.

WHAT ARE MINIMUM WIRE SIZES?

The minimum conductor or wire size to be used should be 16 AWG (1.0 mm^2). This is an ABYC requirement. All cables in any single circuit must always have the same rating. Don't start with one size and splice in another larger or smaller size. I recommend that all wire sizes be standardized to 12-14 AWG (2.5 mm^2) for all general circuits subject to considering the current and volt drop requirements. Cable is cheaper to purchase by the roll.

HOW ARE WIRES CODED OR IDENTIFIED?

In most parts of the world, conductors are identified as red for the positive conductor, and black for the negative conductor. Numbered codes are also an acceptable alternative; the numeral 1 should be used as the positive and the numeral 2 as the negative. Most places in the world modified AC systems coding and moved to IEC standards to avoid confusion, leaving black and red for DC, and brown and light blue for AC. The US do not use these standards and ABYC nominated yellow as a negative polarity color.

HOW TO LABEL WIRES

Always mark cable and wire ends to aid in correct reconnection and troubleshooting. The numbers should match those on your wiring diagram. A simple, slide-on number system can be used. The stick-on types should be avoided as they generally fall off as the adhesive fails. If wires are color-coded, still use numbers, as they are easier and much quicker to identify. The circuit negative should match the positive, and placed in the same sequential order on the negative link.

WHAT TYPE OF CONDUCTOR IS BEST?

Conductors should be stranded and tinned copper. Small boats are exposed to saltwater spray and untinned copper exposed to moisture will very quickly corrode, degrade and fail. Tinned copper is more expensive, but the reliability (and boat resale increase) far outweighs the lower priced plain copper conductor. For some equipment with automatic switches such as bilge and livewell pump circuits, a Triplex wire can be used. Unlike large sail- and powerboats, small fishing boats and their wiring are exposed to the weather much of the time.

HOW TO INSTALL THE WIRING

Connections should be minimized within any circuit between the power supply and the equipment. Connections and joints or splices in cables should be avoided. Any connection adds resistance to a circuit and introduces another potential failure point. Wiring should be neatly installed in as straight a run as practicable. Don't install wiring in bilge areas. Tight bends should be avoided to reduce unnecessary strain on conductors and insulation.

PROTECTING AGAINST MECHANICAL DAMAGE

All wiring should be installed to prevent any accidental damage to the insulation, or cutting of the conductors. This may require protection or covering.

INSTALLING WIRING THROUGH
DECKS AND BULKHEADS

Wiring passing through decks should be protected from damage using a suitable gland, grommet or bushing. The watertight integrity should be maintained. When running wiring through fiberglass holes, don't use a silicon sealant to seal the hole. This usually results in failure, with the cable moving, chafing and damaging the cable. Use circular multi-core cables if possible to ensure proper gland sealing. The Thrudex types are a good choice. Before selecting glands, the structural material of a deck needs to be considered. An aluminum deck requires a different gland to a fiberglass foam sandwich deck.

WHAT SHOULD CABLE CLAMPS MADE OF?

Cable saddles, straps, and cushion clamps should be of a non-corrosive material. The PVC cable tie or tie-wrap is universal in application, and should be used where looms must be kept together, or where any cable can be securely fastened to a suitable support. Do not use cable ties to suspend cables from isolated points as this invariably causes excessive stress and cable fatigue at the tie point. All external cable ties should be the black UV-resistant type.

KEEPING THE WIRES TOGETHER

If a number of wires are lying loose, consolidate them into a neat bundle. Use a length of spiral wrap, and then fasten the loom using cable ties. Another option is the use of split black tubing.

HOW FAR APART SHOULD CABLE CLAMPS BE?

Wires and cables should be supported at maximum intervals of 8" (200mm). The ABYC recommendation is 18" (450mm) apart, but a shorter distance is preferable to secure the cables more efficiently. I have seen far too much movement with the larger spacing distance, and sagging loops develop which are often easy to snag. When cables are run under gunwales of small trailerboats, make sure they are properly secured as they tend to fall down and move when thumping across wave tops.

INSTALLING THE CABLE CLAMPS

Cable saddles should fit neatly, without excessive force onto the cables, or wiring looms, and without deforming the insulation. Cables can be neatly loomed together and secured with PVC or stainless saddles to prevent wiring loom sagging and movement.

INSTALLING HEAVY CURRENT CABLES

Heavy current consumers such as starting motor circuits, trolling motors, windlasses and toilet cables should be installed as far as practicable away from other cables. When large currents flow, interference may be induced or radiated into the other cables. Try and install them on the other side of the boat if possible.

SEPARATING POWER INSTRUMENT CABLES

All wiring should be separated into signal or instrument cables, and DC power supply cables. Where space allows heavy current carrying cables such as trolling motor and outboard starting should also be separated. This is to minimize induced interference between cables, in particular on long, straight parallel runs. All instrument cables should be routed as far as practicable away from power cables.

INSTALLING INSTRUMENT SENSOR CABLES

Instrument cables are generally much smaller than power cables and do not have the same thick and robust insulation. They are easily damaged and care must be taken to avoid damage.

INSTRUMENT AND POWER CABLE CROSSOVERS

Cable crossovers are almost certain. Where instrument cables have to cross power cables, this should be done as close to an angle of 90° as practicable. Induced interference is prevented with right angle crossovers. In addition spacing the cable apart as far as possible with a small air gap is good practice, though it is not easy to do on a small fishing boat.

INSTALLING CABLES EXPOSED TO WEATHER

All externally installed cables should be protected against the effects of ultraviolet (UV) light. Continued exposure to UV on external equipment cables will result in insulation degradation and failure. Small cracks in the insulation allow water to penetrate the conductor and subsequently corrode and degrade the copper. This is common on navigation lights, GPS and radio aerial cables. All exposed cables should be covered in fire retardant black UV resistant spiral wrapping or split loom to prevent rapid degradation of insulation. Cables are also exposed on trailerboats to a range of animals that just love to chew on the wiring during the winter.

LOCATING ELECTRONICS EQUIPMENT CORRECTLY

All navigation electronics equipment, control modules, processors and related components should, if possible, be located clear of cable looms and aerial cables to prevent interference. This should include all radar, cellular telephones, sounders, GPS and VHF. Autopilots are also prone to interference causing major uncontrolled course alterations. An autopilot, severely affected by a cell phone, caused the boat to veer into a breakwater and resulted in fatalities. A minimum distance of 36" (1m) is recommended.

ABOUT CRIMP CABLE TERMINATIONS

All conductors should be terminated where practicable using crimped connectors. Cables terminated within terminal blocks should be secured to prevent contact with adjacent terminals. The most practical and common method of cable connection is the tinned-copper, crimp terminal or connector. These are color coded according to the cable capacity that can be accommodated.

Standard Cable Connectors

Color	AWG	Cable Sizes	Current
Yellow	12–10	3.0–6.0 mm²	30 amps
Blue	16–14	1.5–2.5 mm²	15 amps
Red	22–18	0.5–1.5 mm²	10 amps

QUICK-DISCONNECT (SPADE) CONNECTORS

These are commonly used. Always select the correct quick-disconnect (spade) terminals for the intended cable size. Socket connectors are easily dislodged, and have a tendency to slip off the back of circuit breaker male terminals, so make sure they are tight. For hard duty, look at using heat-shrink fully insulated types. It is important not to apply too much strain on the cables.

IN-LINE CABLE (BUTT) SPLICES

When cables need to be connected and a junction box is not practical, use insulated in-line butt splices. This is more reliable than soldered connections, where a bad joint can cause high resistance and subsequent heating and voltage drop. Use heat shrink insulation over the joint to ensure that waterproof integrity is maintained.

CAN SCREW CONNECTORS BE USED?

Absolutely not. ABYC has a rule against their use. When screw connectors or nuts are used, they screw the cable ends together, fatigue and often break the conductor strands, causing high resistance, heating and failure.

MAKING CRIMP WIRE TERMINATIONS

When crimping use a quality ratchet-type crimping tool. Do not use the cheap squeeze types, which do not adequately compress and capture the cable, subsequently causing failure as the cable pulls out of the connector sleeve. Cable ends should have the insulation removed from the end, without nicking the cable strands. The bare cable strands should be simply twisted together, and inserted in the terminal block or connector of a similar size. Make sure there are no loose strands. Stray strands often cause short circuits with adjacent terminals. A good joint requires two crimps. Always crimp both the joint and the plastic behind it. Make sure that no cable strands are hanging out. Poor crimping is a major cause for failure. After crimping, give the connector a firm tug to ensure that the crimp is sound

ABOUT SOLDER TERMINATIONS

Do not solder the ends of wires prior to connection. In most cases, this is done to make a good low resistance connection and prevent cable corrosion, but the soldering is poorly done with a high resistance joint being made. A soldered cable end also prevents the connector screw from spreading the strands and making a good electrical contact, and causes high resistance and heating.

MAKING CONNECTIONS IN WET LOCATIONS

When connections are made in an area open to spray and water the connections should be suitably protected against water ingress. Joints should be finished with self-amalgamating tapes, or apply some heat shrink tubing, preferably both. I have frequently seen connections for bait tank pumps and float switches permanently wet or immersed in bilges. They all fail.

LIGHTNING AND SMALL BOATS

Like the golfer, the fisherman in a small boat out on a lake is exposed. Many fishermen use graphite and titanium rods, which are an ideal conductive target. How far away is the lightning? Time the lightning flash by counting the number of seconds to when the thunder is heard. Divide this number of seconds by 7 to give the distance in kilometers. Lightning consists of a number of components with charges exceeding 200,000 amperes at over 30,000°C for a matter of milliseconds. The positively charged ions rise to the cloud top, and the negative ions migrate to the cloud base. Regions of positive charged ions also form at the cloud base. Eventually the cloud charge levels have sufficient potential difference between ground and another cloud to discharge. The leader is a negative stream of electrons consisting of many small forks that follow and break down the air paths offering the least resistance. The upward positive leader charge rises some 150 yards (50m) above the ground, and when they meet a channel is formed. The return stroke is generally much brighter and travels upwards to the cloud, partially equalizing the potential difference between ground and cloud. In a matter of milliseconds after the return stroke, another downward charge takes place following the same path as the stepped leader and return stroke.

ABOUT LIGHTNING PROTECTION

In an aluminum boat, the hull acts as a ground plane. In many cases lying down is hard and even with rods lowered the boat and people are still at risk. I have installed a simple aluminum rod some 6 to 8 feet high that slots into the rowlock or similar holder. The rod has a pointed end, and grounds to the boat hull. If there is a strike, this will ground out the energy and give some protection. Fiberglass boats are different, and again where there is a risk, a similar rod mounted in the boat center is suggested. Clamps on temporary ground such as those from Strikeshield may be a viable method. Clamp on to the rod, drop the cable and special ground plate over the side.

ABOUT SMALL BOAT CORROSION

Galvanic corrosion is the process that occurs when galvanic cells form between two pieces of metal with different electrochemical potential when they come into contact or are placed in an electrolyte (saltwater). The difference in electrical potential between the two pieces of metal generates a measurable current flow between the metals. The metal with the lowest potential will corrode. It is called the anode; the one with the higher potential is called the cathode. Corrosion will occur in either salt- or freshwater and the principles are the same. Salinity and water temperature influence the rate of corrosion. Aluminum alloy outboards, trim tabs and trolling motors are the most at risk.

ABOUT METAL NOBILITY

All metals can corrode, both ferrous and non-ferrous. Base metals such as steel and aluminum corrode more easily than the noble metals such as stainless steel and bronze. Metals are classified according to molecular structure and these characteristics are listed in a metallic nobility table. The base metals at the top of scale conduct easily, while the noble metals at the bottom do not. The materials with the greatest negative value will tend to corrode faster than those of a lesser potential. The voltage difference between metals will drive current flow to accelerate corrosion of the anodic metal. When a metal high in the nobility table is connected with one of low nobility, a current will be generated. Zinc is very low in the table and will react with most other metals, which is why zinc anodes are used on boats. For example, a downrigger wire is made of stainless steel, which is high in the table. The reaction between the wire and zinc will have approximately 0.9 volt differential in salt water.

Metal Nobility Table

Metal	Voltage
Magnesium	- 1.65 V
Zinc	- 1.10 V
Iron	- 1.05 V
Aluminum	- 0.75 V
Mild steel	- 0.70 V
Lead	- 0.55 V
Copper, brass and bronze	- 0.25 V
Monel	- 0.20 V
Stainless steel	- 0.20 V
Silver	- 0.00 V
Gold	+ 0.15 V

WHAT IS ELECTROLYTIC CORROSION?

Electrolytic corrosion is caused by an external DC current source such as an electrical leakage or fault on the boat. It is mainly caused by leakage across condensation or conductive salt deposits at DC connections or junction boxes, or tracking from main starter motor cables. 24- and 36-volt systems have higher risks than 12-volt systems, given the higher potential differences. In some cases, they may also be caused by damaged insulation. In a properly installed electrical system, there are relatively few opportunities for the situation to arise. Protective measures for galvanic corrosion do not protect against electrolytic corrosion and electrical leakage or stray currents may waste the anodes very quickly.

ABOUT ZINC ANODE INSTALLATION

Anode positioning is not critical but you must be able to see the parts to be protected. The size and number of zincs used is proportional to the surface area of metal being protected. When a zinc anode is 50–75% wasted it must be replaced. White or green halos around zincs or metals indicate that stray current is affecting them. Never paint the zinc anode. In many fiberglass boats the zinc is fitted to the transom but not bonded to anything. It must be connected to the bonding system.

ABOUT GROUNDING AND BONDING
ON SMALL BOATS

It is important to understand why items are grounded or bonded. The DC negative is not a ground, but a conductor which carries the same current that flows within the positive DC conductor. The instrument ground, which most GPS and radar sets have, is nominally boat ground. In many cases, a complete separate ground terminal link is installed behind the switchboard to which the cable screens and ground wires are connected. A separate large low resistance cable is then taken to the same ground point as other grounds. Do not simply interconnect to the local DC negative to the link as equipment may be subject to interference. The bonding system is used to interconnect equipment and maintain them at equal potential. In small boats this is also used to ground out any static. Fuel tanks are bonded to ground out any static charges that may cause a spark. Trolling motors and outboards are grounded to reduce stray currents and maintain an equal ground plane between them. Through hulls are bonded along with a zinc anode as part of galvanic corrosion protection. Not all through hulls require grounding. Trim tabs are grounded as part of a galvanic corrosion protection system.

WHY IS CIRCUIT PROTECTION REQUIRED?

The heart of all electrical systems is the fuse panel, which allows control, switching and protection of circuits. Switches are used to isolate voltage from circuits as part of normal control. Protection is required to prevent overload currents arising in excess of the cable rating. They are also to protect the cables and equipment from excessive currents that arise during short circuit conditions. Circuit protection is not normally rated to the connected loads, although this is commonly done on loads that are considerably less than the cable rating, such as GPS and VHF radios. The two most common circuit protective devices are the fuse and the circuit breaker.

THE BASIC ELECTRICAL WIRING DIAGRAM

Every electrical circuit is basically the same. A wiring diagram is all of these separate circuits placed together. You can install either fuse and switch or circuit breaker. The positive should go as directly as possible to equipment without connections. The negative should go back to the negative bus and match the same circuit number. The fuse or circuit breaker rating must protect the cable, not the equipment.

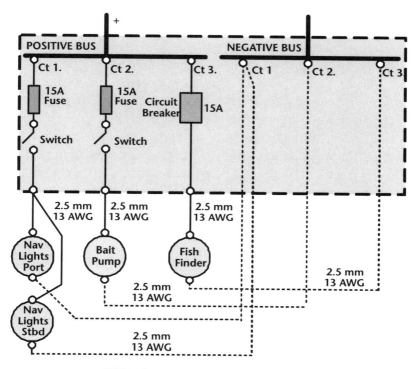

TYPICAL CIRCUIT DIAGRAM

WHAT IS A SHORT CIRCUIT?

A short circuit is where two points of different electrical potential are connected, that is positive to negative. There is what is often called a dead short circuit and an impedant short circuit. Dead short circuits are where the positive and negative are directly connected together without any resistance between them. This is actually rare and will occur when circuits are connected incorrectly, mostly in a new installation. Impedant short circuits are the most common. A typical example is a breakdown across a terminal block.

WHAT IS AN OVERLOAD?

An overload condition is where the circuit current carrying capacity is exceeded by the connection of excessive load. Excessive load can come from too many devices or equipment such as pumps with higher than normal mechanical loads.

ABOUT CIRCUIT BREAKERS

Circuit breakers are the most reliable and practical method of circuit protection. They are manufactured in press button, toggle type, or rocker switch. The term trip free is used to describe a breaker that cannot be held closed when it has tripped. It is an ABYC requirement. Circuit breakers are either magnetic or thermal (bimetallic). Ideally they are used for the circuit isolation and protection, combining both functions. This saves switch panel space, costs and installation time as well as improving reliability. Single pole circuit breakers are normally fitted to boats.

CIRCUIT BREAKERS
Courtesy Blue Sea and ETA

HOW TO SELECT CIRCUIT BREAKERS

Circuit breakers must be selected for the cable size that they protect. The rating must not exceed the maximum rated current of the conductor. The cable sizes in the table give recommended ratings for single circuits.

Circuit Breaker Selection Table

Circ Mils	AWG	mm²	Current
3260	15	1.5 mm²	7.9–15.9 A
5184	13	2.5 mm²	15.9–22.0
8226	1	4.0 mm²	22.0–30.0
13087	9	6.0 mm²	30.0–39.0
20822	7	10.0 mm²	39.0–54.0
33088	5	16.0 mm²	54.0–72.0
52624	3	25.0 mm²	72.0–93.0
66358	2	35.0 mm²	93.0–117.0
105625	0	50.0 mm²	117.0–147.0

HOW DOES A FUSE WORK?

A fuse is essentially a strip of low melting point alloy within a housing that is placed in series with a circuit. When the current increases under load and exceeds the rating of the strip, it blows. This happens during an overcurrent event such as an overload or short circuit. The fuse element melts, ruptures or blows. If you place the multimeter set on the resistance or ohms range, a good fuse reads zero or short circuit. When blown it reads a high, infinite resistance or open circuit.

WHAT TYPES OF FUSES ARE USED?

The most common type of fuse is the simple glass fuse. The AGC and GMA (Buss) 1.25-inch glass type fuses have a wire type element. They are typically found in many in-line fuse holders and screw out fuse holders. The voltage and rating is stamped on the fuse end cap. The AGU fuses have a thin flat fuse element, and the MDL Slow-Blow fuse has a thin spiral type element. The ATO/ATC and ATM fuses are the automotive blade type contained within color coded plastic fuse holders.

They commonly use aluminum fuse elements that tend to corrode quickly and they are not approved by ABYC. Replace with tinned copper types for reliability. The MAXI fuse is a larger version of the ATM types. The ATO type is rapidly replacing the glass type fuses. Always use water resistant fuse holders to prevent moisture from corroding them. If standard automotive fuses are used they generally corrode in the moist salt laden air. *Never* replace fuses with others of higher ratings. If a fuse blows there is something wrong, the fault must be found and fixed.

Fuse Colors and Ratings

Color	Rating
Orange	15 amps
Green	14 amps
Transparent	13 amps
Yellow	12 amps
Blue	11 amps
Red	10 amps
Brown	7.5 amps
Tan	5 amps
Pink	4 amps
Violet	3 amps
Gray	2 amps
Black	1 amp

FUSE PANEL AND FUSES

LARGE FUSE
Courtesy Blue Sea

WHAT IS A SLOW BLOW FUSE?

Slow blow fuses have an element designed to take longer to blow. This is to prevent nuisance blowing when very short duration or transient overloads occur when equipment starts up or under loads, such as trolling motors and anchor windlasses. For example at 150% overload it takes 100 seconds to blow, at 200% it takes 10 seconds, and at 300% it takes 1 second.

WHAT ARE THE LARGE FUSES USED FOR?

Mega, Class T and ANL fuses are used for larger current ratings. Typical circuits are trolling motors, inverters and windlasses. The fuses are bolted onto studs in a fuse block carrier. The fuses also have an indicator that shows when a fuse is ruptured. They also are required to have insulating and protective covers to meet USCG and ABYC recommendations.

WHAT ARE THE PROBLEMS WITH FUSES?

The typical glass fuse is not always accurate and can rupture as much as 10–50% above or below nominal current rating. Fuse elements can fatigue in service with the fuse element properties altering and subsequently the rated value may alter causing "nuisance" failure. Vibration also causes failure. There is often added contact resistance in the fuse holder between each contact and the fuse ends which commonly causes voltage drops, intermittent supply and heating. When a fuse fails, always assume there is a fault. The newer blade type auto fuses tend to be far more resilient to fatigue and damage and are a good alternative to glass fuses.

ABOUT SWITCH PANEL CIRCUIT PROTECTION

The power supply to the switch panel must have short circuit protection. This is usually a slow blow fuse up to 100-amp rating. Circuit isolation must be installed as close as possible to the battery in both the positive and negative conductors; this is an ABYC requirement, although it is not always possible. The isolator should also be accessible and may be incorporated within a single trip free circuit breaker. The isolator must be rated for the maximum current of the starting circuit. Fuses can be used; however it is often better to combine isolation and protection within one easily re-settable device.

ABOUT NAVIGATION LIGHT CIRCUITS

If you are fishing in navigable waterways you will have display lights in accordance with the requirements of the International Regulations for Preventing Collisions at Sea, 1972 and local or national rules. Each circuit should be protected by fuse or circuit breaker. Wire sizes must be rated with a maximum voltage drop of 3–5%. With a circuit breaker supplying all navigation lights, there is the risk of a single fault tripping the breaker and all lights being unavailable until the fault is cleared. This may not be possible in bad weather conditions. Where possible, separate circuit breakers or fuses should be used. On most small trailer boats this is not normal. Alternatively where a single breaker is used, each circuit should have a replaceable fuse and switch installed.

SELECTING AND INSTALLING ISOLATORS

The isolator is usually a switch. It is recommended that you use quality single pole isolators. When 2-position selector switches are used, use caution when installing cheap imported isolators that look like the name brands. I have had many failures on these copies, and installing quality will pay dividends. If you lose the main isolator you lose everything so reliability is essential.

ABOUT BUSBARS AND TERMINAL BLOCKS

All fuses, distribution busbars, and terminals must be covered. The insulation covers should be fitted over all positive and negative busbars, distribution busbars and fuse holders. This is a requirement of the ABYC and protects against accidental contact and water.

WHAT IS THE PURPOSE OF A VOLTMETER?

A voltmeter will also tell you if the battery is charging at the correct voltage level. As a battery has a range of approximately one volt from full charge to discharge condition, accuracy is crucial. Analog voltmeters are the most common. Digital voltmeters are also common and are far more accurate. There are a number of types, including Liquid Crystal Displays (LCD) and Light Emitting Diodes (LED). Where one voltmeter is used to monitor two or more batteries, switching between batteries to voltmeter is through a double pole, center off toggle switch or a multiple battery rotary switch. The sense cable should go directly back to the battery, although on service battery connections most connect directly to the switchboard busbar. Switch off the meter after checking.

WHAT IS THE PURPOSE OF AN AMMETER?

An ammeter is used to monitor the discharge current rate from the house or trolling motor battery or in the charging circuit to monitor the charging current. Ammeters should be selected on the calculated operating range. Shunt ammeters are also used in these applications. Cheaper ammeters are of the series type with the cable under measurement passing through the meter. There is often a very long cable run with resultant voltage drops in the charging circuit, and if the meter malfunctions damage can occur.

WHAT IS A SHUNT AMMETER?

A shunt simply allows the main current to flow through a resistance. This produces a voltage drop and this millivolt value is in direct proportional ratio to the current flowing. The rating or ratio of a shunt will be given in the mV to Amp ratio, i.e. 50mV/50A, meaning that 50mV will equal 50 amps. The meter reads the millivolt value and is displayed on an amp scale. The advantage is that only two low current cables are required to connect the ammeter to the shunt. Install a shunt in the line wherever practical and run sense wires back to the panel mounted meter. Always connect the meter leads to the special connection screws.

ABOUT SMART METERS

Unlike starting batteries, house battery charge levels cycle up and down, and power level information is critical in determining charging periods. Typical of integrated monitors is the E-meter (Link 10). These are "intelligent" devices in that they monitor current consumption, charging current, and a range of monitoring functions that also include voltage, high and low voltage alarms, amp-hours used and amp-hours remaining and allowing the battery net charge deficit to be displayed. The system maintains accuracy by taking into account charging efficiency. The charging efficiency factor (CEF) is nominally set at 87%, with the factor being automatically adjusted after each recharge cycle. A falling CEF is indicative of battery degradation. In addition the E-meter also contains an 'n' algorithm for calculation of Peukerts Coefficient. A meter shunt (500A/500mV) is installed in the negative load line. This is connected by twisted pair wires to prevent noise from induced voltages being picked up and carried into the meter corrupting the data.

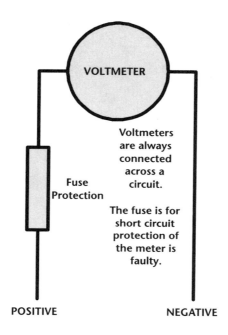

VOLTMETER

Voltmeters are always connected across a circuit.

The fuse is for short circuit protection of the meter is faulty.

Fuse Protection

POSITIVE   **NEGATIVE**

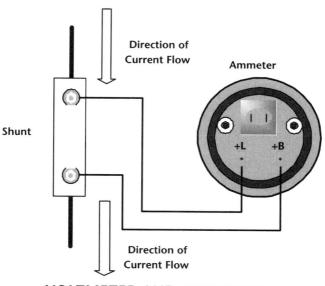

Direction of Current Flow

Ammeter

Shunt

+L   **+B**

Direction of Current Flow

VOLTMETER AND AMMETERS

CIRCUIT BREAKER TRIPS/FUSE
BLOWS WHEN SWITCHED ON

The ammeter will go to off-the-meter full-scale deflection immediately, indicating a high fault current:

- **Load Short Circuit.** Check out the appropriate connected load and disconnect the faulty item before resetting.
- **Connection Short Circuit.** After disconnection of the load the fault still exists. Check cable connections for short circuit, or for cable insulation damage.

CIRCUIT BREAKER TRIPS/FUSE BLOWS
SEVERAL SECONDS AFTER SWITCH ON

The ammeter will slowly rise to an off-the-meter full-scale deflection indicating an increasing high current:

- **Motor is Seized.** The electric motor has seized, or the bearings have seized.
- **Load Seized or Stalling.** Usually due to a seized pump, again usually bearings.
- **Insulation Leakage.** Usually due to a gradual breakdown in insulation, such as wet area connection.

THERE IS NO POWER AFTER
CIRCUIT BREAKER SWITCH ON

- **Circuit Connection.** Check that the circuit connection has not come off the back of the circuit breaker. Check the cable connection to the crimp connection terminal.
- **Circuit Breaker Connection.** On many switch panels, the busbar is soldered to one side of all fuses or circuit breakers. Check that the solder joint has not come away. Some breakers have a busbar that is held under breaker screw terminals; check that the screws and connections are tight.
- **Circuit Breaker.** Operate the breaker several times. In some

cases the mechanism does not make proper electrical contact and several operations will often solve this.

- **Circuit Negative.** Verify that the positive supply voltage is present. Check that the circuit negative wire is secure in the negative link.

INSTALLING AUXILIARY CIRCUITS

The power supply to auxiliary equipment connected directly to the battery must have short circuit protection and circuit isolation installed close to the battery in both the positive and negative conductors. These auxiliary supplies generally include high current equipment such as trolling motors, electric windlasses, etc. connected directly to a battery. A circuit breaker or fuse rated for the cable should be installed as close as possible to the battery, and be accessible. It should also be mounted as high as practicable above possible wet areas. Avoid running smaller circuits and equipment off batteries as control and monitoring is much harder to achieve.

ABOUT BAIT/LIVEWELL PUMP AND AERATOR WIRING

Bait and livewell pumps supply cool and oxygenated water to keep bait or catch fish alive. Aerators circulate and oxygenate water tanks. Like bilge pumps they must have the proper sized cables installed to the pump motor, with watertight electrical connections. Some units also have timer functions. You can keep your bait or catch fresh and alive without worrying about excessive battery drain. When on cycle it pumps for 30 seconds, off cycle is variable from 0 to 5½ minutes. Units also have a continuous run option for filling the livewell. A three wire installation replaces the standard on/off switch.

ABOUT BILGE PUMP WIRING

A bilge pump automatic circuit is controlled by a 2-position and center off switch. In position 1 the power is applied directly to the bilge pump. In position 2 the power is supplied to a float or other switch. When the water level is low and the switch is not activated, power goes to one side of the switch. When water rises and the switch activates and closes, power is then taken directly to the pump. The correctly rated switch must be installed for the pump. Bilge pump wiring must be waterproof and located above maximum water levels. Where an automatic float switch system is used, a red light to show when it runs is useful. Each pump must have a separate circuit and fuse or circuit breaker, do not connect in series, which is a common mistake.

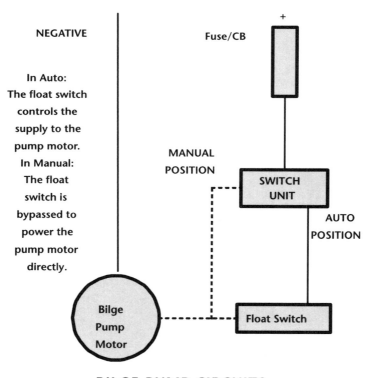

BILGE PUMP CIRCUITS

INSTALLING ELECTRIC POT PULLERS

Some boats use electric pot pullers for crab, shrimp and lobster pot re-trieval. The Robinson Retriever suits the small trailer fishing boat and has a 65 ft/min, 75-lb capacity and draws a maximum of 8.5 amps. The system is compatible with Scotty downrigger mounting and electrical systems. Systems such as the larger capacity EZ-Pull are powered by a 12-volt, 1.3 hp DC motor. The 110 ft/min, 135-lb units draw 42-44 amps, and cables require 50 map circuit breakers. Higher output 135 ft/min, 130-lb units draw up to 50–54 amps and both use quick disconnect plugs. Pot pullers require connection to deep cycle batteries. Volt drop will affect performance so cable sizes must be sized correctly to get best performance. The power consumption should be factored into battery planning.

ABOUT EXTERNAL WIRING INSTALLATIONS

In some cases navigation lights and instrument aerials are installed and mounted on stainless steel structures. The wiring is run through the deck and the cable internally within the stainless tubing. The two main failure points are where the cables run through the deck and where cables enter and exit the stainless tubing. Many deck cable glands are located where the cables and gland can be trodden on, causing mechanical stress and damage. Always place them as far behind tubing base fittings as possible. In many fiberglass boats this is difficult as the deck to hull joint is located in the same location and is limited by below deck cable access. Where cables enter and exit, they should be protected by a sleeve or grommet. A common cause of failure is cable and insulation damage from sharp edges on the holes drilled into the stainless steel tubing. As previously mentioned, apply UV protective coverings to exposed cables.

PROTECTING CABLES AGAINST UV

All exposed cables should be covered in black UV resistant spiral wrapping to prevent rapid degradation of insulation. Small cracks in the insulation allow water to penetrate the conductor and subsequently corrode the copper. This should be applied where a cable exits the mast to a light fitting.

TUNA TOWER CABLES INSTALLATION

When running tuna tower electrical and electronics cables, these are usually installed within the stainless tubing structure. There are often cable faults when the wires are cut or chafe on sharp edges where they enter or exit the tubing. Another unseen hazard are the sharp edges where tubing is joined, so always use quality double insulated tinned cables.

ABOUT 115/230 VOLT AC POWER ON TRAILERBOATS

Very few fishing boats have permanent AC circuits on board. In most cases the battery charger may be permanently installed and connected by plug and lead when required. In general no grounding of the boat is required as the ground path is provided by the lead. Do not remove the ground pin from the extension lead plug. Where AC is required on fishing expeditions for recharging the batteries, a small portable Honda generator is ideal. Honda has integrated the special multi-pole alternator within the engine and an inverter to produce a perfect sine wave AC output. These units have very low noise, rated at around 58 dB. Ratings are typically for the 120V, 1000W unit 8.3A maximum and 900W, 7.5A continuous. For many larger chargers the 2kW or 3kW are more suited.

ABOUT AC POWER SAFETY

Most boats are parked in the yard or driveway and an electric cable is run out to the battery charger. For safety always install a GFCI outlet at the house or garage, and supply the power from there. I have seen faulty equipment and leads on aluminum boats make the hull alive, creating a serious shock hazard, especially to kids playing out in the yard.

INVERTERS ON SMALL FISHING BOATS

Inverters turn DC battery power (12–48 volts) into AC power (120v 60Hz or 230V 50 Hz). They are used to power notebook computers, power tools, camcorders, TV, DVD and appliances (coffee pot). Inverter output waveforms are either square wave, modified share wave (quasi-sine) or a sine wave. Square wave units suit resistive load equipment such as incandescent lights and heating equipment. Modified square wave inverters will power most equipment, although microwaves do not run as efficiently. Sine wave will power everything efficiently.

ABOUT INVERTER POWER RATINGS AND EFFICIENCY

Inverters have two ratings, continuous and surge or intermittent rating. The continuous rating is the power it can handle all the time. Surge ratings are important as some loads such as motors require an instantaneous current at start of 3–6 times the normal run current. If the inverter rating is too low the current overload may cause the unit to shut down. The efficiency of newer lightweight high frequency units can be as high as 94%. Some inverters consume power at idle or standby. The amount varies from 300 mW to 5–10% of rated output, others are load sensed and shutdown automatically when not in use. How much power does the inverter take? A good guide is 0.9 amps for every 10 watts of load. Example: 300 watts requires 27.5 amps DC; 1000 watts = 91 amps. If powering off the trolling motor deep cycle batteries, 12 or 24 volts, the battery size should increase or the available trolling capacity and period will be seriously reduced.

INSTALLATION NOTES FOR INVERTERS

Many fishing boats have a cigarette lighter plug in units which handle small loads of 50 to 300 watts, although this is often too much for outlet at full load. Many smaller inverters also use clips for the battery terminals. These tend to cause voltage drop and hard wiring is preferable. Where large output units are used, install heavy duty cabling and the same volt drop rules apply as for trolling motors. The supply cable from the battery must be protected by a fuse or breaker. Class T fuses are usually used. The AC grounding must be carried out in accordance with the installation instructions. Install the inverter in a clean and dry location as the risk for an electrical shock exists.

ABOUT US BOAT TRAILER WIRING

Trailer lighting is critical. Most light fittings are vehicle types with incandescent lamps. They are easily flooded and waterlogged, with resulting burnout and failure. The new LED types have lower heat outputs and can be potted or sealed to reduce water ingress when launching. There are a number of trailer wiring and plug/socket configurations. The following are standard although you should check your own vehicle to be sure. In the 6-pin terminal plug/socket the center terminal is marked A, and is an auxiliary terminal and is generally used for backup (reverse) lights. It is also used to supply +12 volts to charge the breakaway switch battery, which is common with electric braking on the trailer. In the 7-pin terminal plug/socket 7 is the center terminal.

6 Pin Connector

Marking	Color	Function
GD	White	Ground
TM	Brown	Tail lights
LT	Yellow	Left hand turn
S	Red	Stop/electric brake
RT	Green	Right hand turn
A (Center)	Blue	Auxiliary

7 Pin Connector

Marking	Color	Function
1	White	Ground
2	Blue	Electric brake
3	Green	Tail/run lights
4	Black	Battery charge +
5	Red	Left turn stop
6	Brown	Right turn stop
7 (Center)	Yellow	Auxiliary/back up

It is best to attach the trailer wiring harness ground directly to the trailer frame. The most common failure in trailer electrical systems is a bad ground connection.

Flat 4 Wire Connector

Color	Function
White	Ground
Yellow	Left turn/brake
Green	Right turn/brake
Brown	Tail light

ABOUT AUSTRALIAN TRAILER WIRING CODES

Since 1988 there is a standardized 7-pin system. There are also older 6- and 12-pin connectors in use.

7 pin	Color	Function
1	Yellow	Left hand indicator light
2	Black	Reversing (backup light)
3	White	Ground/earth
4	Green	Right hand indicator light
5	Blue	Service/trailer brakes
6	Red	Stop (brake) light
7	Brown	Tail, license, clearance light
12 pin	**Color**	**Function**
8	Orange	Battery charger/winch
9	Pink	Auxiliaries/battery feed
10	White	Ground/earth

11	Grey	Rear fog light
12	Violet	Spare

ABOUT UK/EUROPEAN TRAILER WIRING CODES

The UK/Europe use ISO Standards with two 7-pin plugs.

12N Socket Standard

Pin	Color	Function
1 (L)	Yellow	Left hand indicator light
2 (54G)	Blue	Rear fog light
3 (31)	White	Ground/earth
4 (R)	Green	Right hand indicator light
5 (58R)	Brown	RHS tail/license plate light
6 (54)	Red	Stop (brake) light
7 (58L)	Black	LHS tail/license plate light

12S Socket Supplementary

Pin	Color	Function
1	Yellow	Reverse light or brake
2	Blue	System
3	White	Spare
4	Green	Return for pin 4
5	Brown	Power auxiliary/battery
6	Red	Warning lamp
7	Black	Refrigerator Return for pin 6

8

SONAR AND FISH FINDERS

INTRODUCTION TO SONAR

The recent developments in computing power and microelectronics have resulted in major advances in SONAR development. I spent a couple of years on new submarine SONAR systems. This defense level capability has now entered the fishing world. The term SONAR is derived from the words SOund NAvigation Ranging.

HOW DOES SONAR WORK?

An electrical signal is sent to the transducer. The electrical signal to energize the transducer crystal is generated by an amplifier. The energized crystal reverberates at a particular frequency, to convert the electrical signal into mechanical acoustic or sound energy. The acoustic energy causes oscillation of the water molecules through which the sound travels. The sound is pulsed out in a defined beam. These beams travel out in a wave pattern. The acoustic pulse travels through the water at a rate of approximately 4800 ft (1500m) per second in saltwater and 4920 ft/sec in fresh water. When the energy strikes an object within that beam such as fish, some of the energy is reflected, or echoed back to the transducer. The transducer collects this return and processes it into a signal. The processor is programmed with the rate of sound transmission in the water, and calculates the time difference between the transmission and reception of the returned signal to give a range or depth figure. This result is then displayed as a number or as an image on a screen. Freshwater and saltwater tend to absorb and scatter sound signals, and the higher frequencies are more susceptible than lower frequencies. Water is frequently being mixed due to environmental factors such as wind and wave actions. The water has air bubbles, suspended materials such as silt, minerals and salts that vary in quantity. There are also micro-organisms that include plankton and algae, all which scatter, absorb and reflect sonar signals.

WHAT ARE WE LOOKING FOR?

The depth determines the fishing technique, and what type of lure or bait. The fishfinder lets you see who may be at home down there, but it will not guarantee a catch. That part is up to your skills. In most fishing you will be looking for underwater structure, such as tree stumps, ledges and significant bottom changes. Cover consists of underwater object such as tree stumps, weed beds, logs, etc. You may also be looking for gullies and channels or break-lines, which constitute a sharp bottom drop off point. You may just be looking for fish activity. If you locate a tight ball of bait fish, they are probably being chased by a predator. A loose school indicates no activity. A fish finder is not necessarily going to tell you what the fish is. Interpretation involves understanding both the underwater features and fish behavior to distinguish between bait fish and the target fish. Distinguishing between bass and shad or other species is the angling part.

ABOUT SONAR TRANSDUCERS

The transducer is typically constructed of a crystal composed of various elements that include lead zirconate or barium titanate and conductive coatings. When the transducer transmits the acoustic signal, it expands to form a cone shaped characteristic. When the acoustic signal strikes a fish (the fishes air bladder) or seabed, it is reflected back and captured for processing. The shape, thickness and diameter of a transducer crystal determine the cone angle and the frequency. Most sonar systems use round crystals, and the thickness sets the frequency and the diameter sets cone angle. A 194 kHz transducer with a 20-degree cone angle is only around 1 inch (25mm) in diameter. In general the greater the diameter the smaller the cone angle becomes. Methods for converting electrical to acoustical energy are the magnetostrictive, and the ceramic (piezoelectric) methods. The transducer aperture or face is coated with a membrane or surface cover.

WHAT IS A MAGNETOSTRICTIVE TRANSDUCER?

The magnetostrictive transducer uses the principle of magnetostriction. This causes certain materials to expand and contract when they are placed in an alternating magnetic field. This conversion takes place when the material is magnetized causing it to strain. It is a bidirectional process, transmit and receive, used in higher powered low frequency sounders.

WHAT IS A CERAMIC PIEZOELECTRIC TRANSDUCER?

The piezo effect is where certain materials change dimension when an electrical charge is applied to them. An electrical signal is applied to the piezoelectric element in the transducer which then vibrates. The element vibrations are amplified by the resonant transducer masses and then directed into the water through a radiating plate.

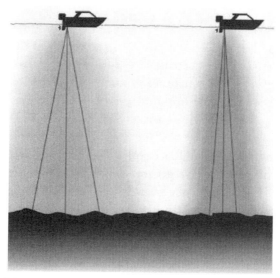

CONE ANGLES—NARROW AND WIDE
Courtesy Lowrance

POWER OUTPUT EFFECT ON BOTTOM RANGE
Courtesy Lowrance

WHAT IS A CONE ANGLE?

The cone angle is based on the power at the center of the cone out to a point where the power decreases to -3db, with the total angle being measured from a -3db point on each side. The further away from the centerline of the cone, the less strong return echoes are. This can be improved by increasing the sensitivity control. Most manufacturers offer models with a variety of cone angles, typically 15–20 degrees. The wider cone angles have less depth capability with wider coverage. The smaller cone angles give greater depth penetration with reduced area coverage. High frequency transducers (190 kHz) are available in either wide or narrow cone angles. Low frequency transducers have cone angles in the range 30–45 degrees. The wide cone angle should be used for most freshwater applications and the narrow cone angle should be used for all saltwater applications. The basic equation is ½ of the cone angle x 3.14 divided by 180 = tangent.

The tangent x depth x 2 = diameter of cone in feet.

If you are fishing in 18 foot of water the 9-degree transducer will be viewing a section of the bottom approximately 2.8 feet in diameter. The 24-degree transducer will cover a bottom area of approximately 7 feet in diameter.

Cone Diameter and Bottom Circles

Depth	9 Degree	12 Degree	19 Degree
10	1.6	2.2	3.4
20	3.2	3.4	6.7
30	4.7	6.3	10.0
40	6.3	8.4	13.4
50	7.9	10.6	16.7
60	9.4	12.6	20.0
70	11.0	14.7	23.4
80	12.6	16.8	26.8
90	14.2	20.0	30.1
100	15.7	21.0	33.5
120	18.9	25.2	40.2
150	23.6	31.5	50.2

WHAT ARE SIDE LOBES?

The actual transmission cone is not clearly defined. The area outside of the nominal cone angle is also able to detect and reflect signals. This depends on the target or echo strength, and the ability of the angler to interpret any images in those areas. The regions outside of the nominal cone angle are called side lobes. The higher quality transducers may have relatively small side lobes. Fishing often requires the advantages of wide and narrow beams. Typically these are a 9- and a 19-degree cone within the single transducer. While most fishfinders have a single beam, manufacturers such as Humminbird have multi-beam systems that have several sonar beams ranging from 2 to 6. This subsequently increases the coverage area, and accuracy. The Single Beam has a cone angle of 16–24 degrees, which gives a depth of 600–1000 feet.

WHAT IS THE DEAD ZONE?

Within the cone coverage there is an area called the dead zone. As a transducer beam angle increases so does the dead zone. The sounder will mark the bottom at the closest point and on a sloping bottom may not show the lower slope or any fish in that lower area. Smaller beam angles reduce this. The sensitivity or gain control allows some adjustment to maximize returns in these areas.

MULTI AND SIDE BEAM SONARS

A switching box is used to switch between them. The Dual Beam system has ranges up to 2000 feet. The first beam is in the cone center, and a second beam surrounds it to increase the coverage area. The Tri-Beam systems have a 90-degree coverage area with ranges up to 1000 feet. The main beam is directed down, and two beams are configured to each side to give a large coverage area. The Wide Side has 3 beams to view bank and bottom contours with the center beam directed down port 120 feet and starboard to 120 feet. The Six Beam system gives a 3D contour display of the sea bottom, and Lowrance systems give coverage of 53 degrees up to a depth of 240 feet. The typical rule is the bottom coverage is approximately one third of the depth. This concept is very important in maximizing the benefit of a fishfinder. The shallower you get the less chance of picking up a fish as the cone coverage area decreases. The sounder may not show what is exactly underneath but what is in the cone angle, so any image may be a few feet either side of the boat.

ABOUT SIDESCAN SONARS

The limitation of basic single beam systems is that the cone is below the transducer. Directing a beam horizontally results in confused returns reflected from waves and bottom. The Bottom Line fish finder has software and filtering that screen out these returns so that the fish are visible. Some units have multi-beam outputs giving side and bottom scanning capability.

WHAT IS TRANSDUCER CAVITATION?

Cavitation, caused by water turbulence passing over a transducer head, affects transducer performance. At slow speeds the laminar flow is smooth without any interference; however at speed air bubbles are created over the transducer face affecting acoustic signal transmission and reception. The effect is to interfere with transmitted acoustic signals that reflect back off the bubbles, which effectively causes noise and masks signals. Turbulence is caused by hull form or obstructions, water flow over the transducer, turbulence from propulsion. Transom mounted units must be carefully mounted to avoid turbulence from outboard motors or water flow off the transom. The higher the speed the greater the turbulence; riveted alloy boats have turbulence off each rivet head. Manufacturers are designing transducers that work better at higher speeds, including transducers with improved hydrodynamic shapes. Transducers must be mounted in areas of little turbulence or clear of hull flow areas, which is not always easy.

SONAR FREQUENCIES

The acoustic transmission frequency affects both the water depth range and the cone angle. The lower frequencies are used in deeper waters and have lower power losses. They also tend to have wider beam angles and cover wider viewing areas. There are many frequencies used in sonar systems. Typical are 38, 40, 50, 75, 107, 120, 150, 192, 200, 400, and 455 kHz. Lowrance have a frequency of 192 kHz transducers with either a wide (20°) or narrow (8°) cone angle, and a deepwater one of 50kHz with a 35° cone angle. Simrad units have a user selectable tri-frequency capability of 38/50, 38/200 or 50/200kHz with depth range up to 1800 meters; they have a maximum ping rate of 15 per second. Shallow waters less than 300 feet give the best results with high frequency transducers of 200kHz and wide cone angles up to 20 degrees. In depths greater than 300 feet low frequency transducers of 50kHz with small cone angles of 8 degrees are the best option.

ABOUT THE POWER OUTPUT OF A FISH FINDER

Power output affects the bottom range capability of a sounder. Deeper water fishing requires higher power outputs. Power outputs are quoted in watts (w), some quote watts peak-to-peak (P-P) however watts RMS is the more accurate. Typically it is in the range 100–600 watts. The basic conversion is P-P watts = RMS watts x 8, i.e. 80 watts RMS = 640 watts P-P. Some have transmission power ratings up to 1000W. A good starting point is around the 600-watt range, and you can go up to 3,000 watts (3kW).

ABOUT THE SENSITIVITY CONTROL

The sensitivity or gain control is used to either "tune in" or "tune out" returns. If the unit is set with low sensitivity it will not detect bottom details, fish or obstruction. If high sensitivity settings are used it will return signals on everything and will clutter the screen with spurious returns or clutter and noise. High sensitivity control settings give you a defined look at structure and cover. When you encounter a lot of suspended material and debris, or heavy cover, a reduction in sensitivity is required. If a fish is inside the transducers' cone, but the sensitivity is not turned up high enough to see it, then you have a narrow effective cone angle. You can change the effective cone angle of the transducer by varying the receivers' sensitivity. With low sensitivity settings, the effective cone angle is narrow, showing only targets immediately beneath the transducer and a shallow bottom. Turning the sensitivity control up increases the effective cone angle, letting you see targets farther out to the sides. The best settings are usually around the 70–80% mark. Experimentation with settings is recommended. Sensitivity should be adjusted so that bottom is clearly defined along with white or gray line and some surface clutter. Most fish finders have automatic sensitivity adjustment, which compensates for ambient water conditions and depth. Lowrance have what is termed Advanced Signal Processing (ASP) which uses complex software to process parameters such as water conditions, noise and interference levels to automatically adjust settings and optimize the display images. This requires setting the sensitivity to the highest level possible without allowing noise to be displayed, thus creating a balance between noise rejection and sensitivity. Acoustics signals are absorbed and reflected. The higher the frequency the greater the scattering effects, and the lower the frequency the greater the range. Wave actions, micro-organisms, varying salt densities and suspended solids further enhance signal scattering. In general the gain goes up with increasing depth and reduces when going shallower.

ABOUT FISH FINDER SCREENS

The three-dimensional (3D) signal transmission and reception is processed to display a two-dimensional (2D) image. The most common display type is the Liquid Crystal Display (LCD), Lowrance have what is called Film SuperTwist and Humminbird use FSTN. Grayscale uses a number of shades of gray to indicate signal strength variations, with strong signals being very dark and weak ones light gray. The LCD display comprises a complex grid or matrix of cells called pixels, which are small square display elements that comprise a screen image. Pixels are turned on or off to form an image on the screen, and return echoes are processed and displayed as dark pixels. A single column of vertical pixels is used that represents the range, the top being the transducer and the bottom being the range setting. When an echo or return is detected one or more pixels in the column are switched on. Each successive return activates a new column of pixels so that a continuous image is displayed on the screen as each column is replaced. The display resolution quality is dependent on the number of pixels in each vertical column. The number of horizontal pixels determines the retention period that a displayed image is on the screen. The scrolling effect is historical in that images are made of sequential returns added together to form a large image of the bottom. The scroll rate is based on a time setting.

WHAT ARE THE LCD SCREEN CHOICES?

Displays must be both high resolution and good contrast and are typically in the range of 240 and 320 vertical pixels. Displays are also sometimes quoted in pixels per square inch, i.e. 15,170, and the more pixels the better the resolution. Many are happy to have a 160 x 160 pixel unit, however the image is a lot sharper with a 240 x 240 pixel screen, and some Grayscale screens have 480 x 350 pixels. Some new units come up to 400 x 400 pixels. If you have a 240-pixel unit set at 240 feet then each foot of depth will equal one pixel. Strong returns will also switch on the adjacent pixels to give a larger image. You may get small images all the way up the column which can be caused by small fish, debris and noise. The full color VGA TFT screens from Lowrance have pixel resolutions of 640 x 480. Humminbird have what they call a high resolution Grayscale Liquid Paper Graph (LPG). Some units have high-resolution displays in 8 or 16 colors on a 10.4-inch TFT LCD display. Color displays use up to 16 colors for different signal strengths. The stronger ones are displayed in red, weaker signals as green or blue, for example bait fish schools are generally in blue or green, with larger game fish being yellow, orange or red. The seabed and wrecks are usually displayed as dark orange or red.

WHAT DOES SPLIT CHART MEAN?

This feature allows an angler to create a window. One screen may be a normal image. The other may have a magnified or zoom image of bottom, structure or a depth range.

WHAT ABOUT IMAGE SIZES?

The image size is not always related to the size of the target. The echo and the image size relate to the time that a fish was detected and stayed within the transducer cone. A large fish passing through the cone quickly will show up as a small target. The strongest returns are always from the seabed. Hard bottoms have a stronger signal return so the images are more solid. Soft bottoms absorb signal so appear as thicker images.

WHAT IS CHART SPEED?

The term was based on earlier paper chart sounders. The faster speeds are preferable. You observe each new line being displayed as the most current so at fast speeds the update rate is faster. When hunting for structure it is best to set the chart speed at maximum and at least the same as the boat speed. This gives you a common reference point without trying to factor in any processing delays.

ABOUT FISH ALARMS

These drive me crazy. Beep! Beep! All day long, like digital watches and cell phones. A sounder cannot distinguish between bass, catfish or rubber boots so the alarm is on every time.

WHAT IS GRAYLINE OR WHITELINE FUNCTION?

All fishfinders have a feature called grayline or whiteline that assists in discriminating bottom hardness from the bottom contours. The bottom is displayed as a thin dark line with a gray area below it. Thin lines and thick well defined gray areas represent hard bottoms. A thick black line with no gray represents soft bottoms as these do not reflect acoustic signals as well. This allows targeting of precise bottom formations for specific fish types. The Grayline(r) feature on Lowrance fishfinders allows differentiation between soft and hard bottom types. The feature "paints" gray on bottom targets that have a stronger signal return than preset values. A soft mud type bottom will have a relatively weak return displayed as a narrow gray line, and hard rock bottoms will have a strong return represented with a wide gray line, with the gray always having the strongest signal.

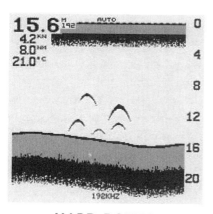

HARD BOTTOM   SOFT BOTTOM
Courtesy of Lowrance

HOW DOES THE ZOOM FUNCTION WORK?

The zoom setting is a really useful tool. You can zoom in on any specific range, or bottom to get a close up view. The zoom function allows the magnification of a portion of the depth range to improve analysis and identification of targets in that area. The typical magnification scales are x2 and x4 the normal scale. This allows monitoring of a certain depth range such as 40 to 50 feet, or zooming on the bottom and 10 feet above it. The split screen feature allows tracking of different features such as zoom segment and bottom contour.

WHAT IS THE AUTO MODE?

Auto mode allows you to find the structure, bottom or fish you are looking for in the transducer cone coverage area. Leaving your finder in auto mode all the time will not give you the best results. When fishing shallow waters the auto settings are not ideal, and it is better to switch off the function, go to manual and set up for the depth you are fishing in.

SETTING THE UPPER AND LOWER LIMITS

This lets you define a specific area to look at. If you set up at 30 feet as the upper limit and 20 feet as the lower limit, you will be monitoring a 10-feet range between those settings.

WHAT IS FISH ID?

The echo images are replaced with an icon of a fish when processing the signal. This means that every echo is displayed as a fish, including weed, logs, bubbles, thermoclines etc. When you go into the settings menu, you can deselect the fish ID function and you may have to adjust the gain settings.

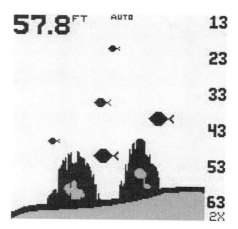

FISH ID SCREEN
Courtesy of Lowrance

ABOUT WATER TEMPERATURE AND THERMOCLINES

Water stratification occurs generally in three layers. The top layer, the epilimnion, is warmer and oxygen enriched from wind action. The second layer is called the metalimnion. The interface between the top layer is called the thermocline and it occurs in the metalimnion. The thermocline area is never uniform. The temperature gradient rapidly decreases with depth. Thermoclines are important to locating fish as they tend to be found either just above or below them. The bottom layer is called the hypolimnion,. It is low in oxygen, nutrients and is cold. These layers are changing continuously, and are affected by the action of surface heating, wind and waves. Sometimes another layer forms below the hypolimnion. It is called an oxygen inversion which is fed by underwater springs. Fish finders can detect a thermocline and the greater the difference in temperatures the more visible it becomes. This is where bass and bait fish are often found. There are clear differences between seasons and when large water inflows occur in lakes. It is important to understand lake dynamics if you are to get the best fishing results.

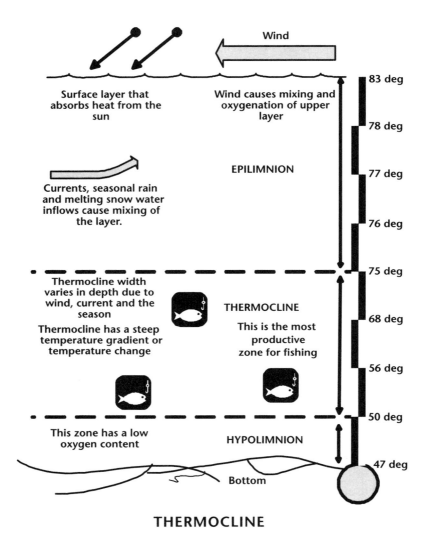

THERMOCLINE

HOW FISH ARCHING OCCURS

The display of fish arches on the screen is directly related to sonar acoustic characteristics, sensitivity adjustments, boat speed, water depth and cone angle, and location of the fish within the cone. As a fish enters the acoustic cone a display pixel is turned on. As it moves towards the center of the cone the distance between the transducer and fish decreases so that pixels are progressively turned on and display a shallower depth and therefore a stronger signal. When the fish reaches the cone center this forms half the arch, and the other half is completed as the fish moves towards the outer edge of the cone. Very small fish will probably not arch at all. Because of water conditions such as heavy surface clutter or thermoclines, the sensitivity sometimes cannot be turned up enough to get fish arches. For the best results, turn the sensitivity up as high as possible without getting too much noise on the screen. If the fish does not pass through the cone center the arch will either be partial or not be displayed. Arches are not formed in shallower waters as the cone angle becomes too narrow. Fish schools vary in displayed shape depending on how much of the school is within the cone. In deeper water each fish if large enough may have an arch displayed. The size of an arch does not relate to the fish size.

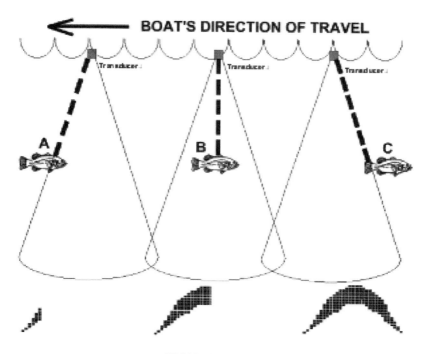

FISH ARCHES

DO SOUNDERS AND OTHER ACOUSTIC
NOISES SCARE THE FISH?

Absolutely! My work on a submarine sonar program showed me how noisy the sea and any body of water can be, full of environmental and biological sound sources. Whales and dolphins communicate using acoustics, the latter as well as porpoise use sonar to hunt. Seals and catfish use their whiskers to detect acoustic activity of their prey. A fish has a series of receptors located along the lateral line, which is comprised of an array of sensory cells and nerve endings. Every acoustic noise generated is detected by the fish on these cells, and this includes the acoustic noise generated by fish as they swim. This is caused by water displacement and creation of small ripples or turbulence. Crustaceans and mollusks also create noise that is their downfall as fish locate them. Many fish also know when predators are in the area from the acoustic noise they create. Lure makers now concentrate on adding acoustic effects that mimic natural prey, such as vibrating plugs, poppers and rattle lures, and these along with special flies are used in night fishing. Different fish will have different thresholds of perception. Any fish will have adapted to the ambient or background noise of the habitat, and any unusual or abnormal noise that is not consistent will be detected. Sounder noise tends to be directional and the closer the fish is to the source, the greater the impact. Assume that sounder is detected, and decide when set up on location whether you will switch the sounder off. If it doesn't affect your fishing, stay as you are, but for tournaments everything counts. Boat noise includes the sound of an approaching boat which will produce noise from the outboard motor and the propeller noise signature and cavitation, which is affected by hull form, chines and boat speed. The propeller noise signature is also affected by small blade and tip damage. Noise from inside the boat is also a major factor. The pro tournament fishermen soundproof their boat and keep noise to an absolute minimum. Noise sources also come from bait pumps and bilge pumps, all which may cause vibration and noise on the hull, so they must be carefully mounted on shock absorbent mounts. You have to "run silent," as submarines do. Trolling motors are also a source of noise. When the motor is switched on there is momentary partial cavitation and vibration created by water bubble or cavity formation due to pressure reduction at the rear, tips and faces of the propeller blades. Bearings also create noise; Minn Kota use special bearing systems in trolling motors to reduce noise outputs. A constantly running trolling motor may not spook fish, however sudden large speed increases alter the ambient noise levels with a higher noise output.

ABOUT DEPTH SOUNDERS

The most common depth instrument is for monitoring depth under the boat with a digital, analog or rotating flashing display. These displays have depth alarms, anchor watch alarm facilities, etc. The information displayed is generally 1–3 second old due to signal processing times. The depth sounder transmits a directional sound signal down where it bounces off the bottom, fish or structure and reflects a signal back to the transducer. The signal is processed, with the elapsed time between the signal transmission and reception calculated based on the known sound propagation rate in the water. The result is then displayed.

THE FLASHER DEPTH SOUNDER

The flasher has been around for many years and it is still very popular. Some anglers can interpret the readout and detect fish. The flasher has a large ring and scale. Flashers such as the Vexilar have green for a weak signal, orange for medium returns and flashing red light for strong returns. In some the darker the red blip, the stronger the return or the longer the fish stayed in the cone. Flasher display an image virtually immediately without any processing time delays and are often used at high boat speeds. Flashers are also useful when fishing in areas where the bottom has dense cover such as hydrilla. This is thick underwater vegetation which tends to absorb and give confused reflected signals with unclear images and depth readings on fish finders. Flashers tend to give you true bottom readings. A combination of both often allows calculation of vegetation. Hydrilla forms dense mats right to the surface, thicknesses given some can be as much as 5–10 feet. Flashers also tend to be more effective in very shallow water of just a couple of feet.

ABOUT COMBINATION SOUNDERS

Some manufacturers such as Humminbird have combined the advantages of the flasher sounder with the fish finder. They have what is called a real time sonar (RTS) window located on the right hand side of the screen. The RTS window gives an instantaneous sonar return from the bottom, structure or any fish located within the transducer beam cone. The RTS window gives much faster updates (30 times per second) than the chart window which must do the signal processing. The chart window is a historical log of the sonar signal returns previously displayed in the RTS window. In most bass fishing cases you are searching for bottom contour changes, cover or looking for structure rather than just fish hunting. The dual capability allows this rather than looking at a flasher and separate sounder. Most bass fishing takes place in less than 15 feet (5m) of water. This is often above hydrilla where locating the actual bottom is very important.

ABOUT PAPER CHART RECORDERS

These sounders were the first types on the market. They use a pen or stylus to etch the images on a special sensitized paper. This passes an electrical current through a conductive paper to the back plate to burn on the image. There are still many anglers who prefer these as they are very sensitive and give good images. Keep the paper warm and dry!

READ THE INSTRUCTION MANUAL!

Many fishfinder problems are due to incorrect operation. Read the manual and practice using the finder. Understand how to navigate through the various menus and options. If you have lost the manuals you can get most off websites. Lowrance, Eagle and Humminbird have most available for free download.

WHAT IS SOUNDER KEEL OFFSET?

This adjustment is important so that the depth of the water under the boat hull bottom is measured accurately. Many installations have this inaccurately set and often run needlessly aground. Read the manual and adjust this accurately.

HOW ACCURATE IS THE DEPTH SOUNDER?

Acoustic signals suffer from propagation delays and attenuation as water and various bottom formations cause absorption, scattering, refraction and reflection. Biological matter such as algae and plankton as well as suspended particulate matter like silt, dissolved minerals and salts can cause this. The water density and salinity levels as well as water temperatures all affect signal propagation. Bottom formations consisting of sand and mud or large quantities of weed beds will absorb or scatter signal; hard bottoms that comprise shale, sand and rock will reflect signal with strong returns. The power output of a unit is also important with respect to range and resolution, the higher the power the greater the depth range and signal return.

MOUNTING THE DISPLAY UNIT

The fish finder should be mounted on a swivel base in an area of good visibility if used for both navigation and fishing. When a dedicated unit is used, mounting the display for easy viewing from your fishing position is best. This is usually up forward with the transducer mounted on the trolling motor. Cabela sell a range of screen neoprene covers for most makes and models.

MOUNTING THROUGH HULL TRANSDUCERS

Mounting through hull transducers requires a hole in the hull. The transducer is mounted through the hull using a threaded shaft and nut. It must be correctly aligned in the fore and aft position. Be very careful not to bump the transducer and possibly damage the crystal element. The transducer must be at least 1 foot forward of the outboard and have smooth, turbulence and cavitation free water flow over it at all times. The trailer must not strike and tear off the transducer, so check and measure trailer supports. The transducer is mounted as deep in the water as possible given the boats hull form, as this reduces cavitation and turbulence problems. Fairing blocks must be used with a hull having a deadrise greater than 10 degrees. These are made from plastic or timber and shaped so that the transducer will be vertical and the face pointing directly downwards. When mounting in an aluminum hull, select plastic transducers to avoid any galvanic corrosion problems. Route the transducer cable as far as practicable from other electrical cables to avoid interference.

MOUNTING INBOARD TRANSDUCERS

Shoot through the hull type transducers are very common and recommended only for the 192 and 200 kHz transducers. This type of mounting eliminates the cavitation problem and also the risk of mechanical damage. The sound is transmitted and received through the boat hull. There can be significant reductions in signal strength and therefore depth ranges if not done properly. You can't use this with aluminum hulls and sandwich hulls can cause some problems. The transducer should be mounted inside the hull towards the transom. It should be clear of stringers and frames and as close to the centerline as possible in an area of solid fiberglass. In sandwich hulls you will have to remove the top layer and mount it against the outer layer. The transducer is fastened using epoxy resin. Water is allowed to surround the transducer. If the performance is not as expected, there is probably air under the transducer head, or the gelcoat has an air bubble in it. Route the transducer cable as far as practicable from other electrical cables to avoid interference.

MOUNTING TRANSOM TRANSDUCERS

The most common installation method on many small fishing boats is the use of transom mounting transducers. These are installed on retractable brackets, most of which kick up when contacting objects. They are susceptible to turbulence from the propeller. The laminar water flow breaking away from the hull can often affect operation, and it is most effective at low boat speeds. Mount the transducer on the transom, and locate in a position between rows of rivets, as water flow and turbulence over the rivets may affect accuracy. There should be a minimum of 1 inch (25mm) between the transducer and transom. The transducer should also be mounted as deep in the water as possible.

When it is mounted, adjust the bracket so that the rear trailing edge is slightly lower than the forward pointed end, the angle is about 2–5 degrees down. Depending on how the boat rides when under way, you have to look at whether the bow rides higher or level with the transom. When moving the boat on and off trailers caution should be used. Route the transducer cable away from other electrical cables to avoid interference. In many cases the loose cables get fouled and damaged. It is a good idea to use a dedicated mounting plate on aluminum boats, such as the Cabela unit. You may need to do some trial runs on the water and adjust it a few times to get it just right.

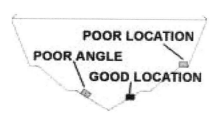

TRANSOM MOUNTINGS

TROLLING MOTOR TRANSDUCER MOUNTINGS

Many boats mount the transducer on the trolling motor. The first factor is the right transducers. These are commonly "puck" style transducers. The critical point when mounting is the cable installation. The cable must be installed so that it doesn't foul the trolling motor and cannot be damaged, cut or pulled out. The simplest method of installation is to use black PVC cable ties at the bottom and leave the cable slack to the top. Hose clamps are not so successful and do not have the give of PVC ties. Clip the cable tie off at the ratchet point, and make sure that nothing can catch on the remaining protrusion. Wrap a layer of insulation of self-amalgamating tape over the tie to prevent any snagging. Route cables well clear of supply cables and radio aerials, or next to speed/log cables. If you bundle them together they will induce interference.

LOOKING AFTER THE TRANSDUCERS

The most common cause of sounder problems is the transducer mechanical damage. The greatest damage occurs while being moved on and off the trailer, or while being towed on the road. Gravel, debris, mud, dirt and other road material get whipped up striking the transducer. Oil and dirt reduce the transducer sensitivity and can even prevent operation. The bottom of the transducer should be washed regularly with soap and water to take off any oil film and dirt. I use one of those green kitchen pot scrubbing pads and dish washing liquid soap. Tar is best removed using one of the common vehicle tar removers. Once tar is removed wash with liquid soap again. The best method is prevention, wrap the transducer before travelling. I prefer plastic bubble wrap and Duck or gaffer duct tape. Make sure you remember to remove it when going in the water. If your boat is left in the water most of the time check the surface for marine growth. Avoid applying normal antifouling to the transducer surface, as it includes small voids and air bubbles, which will reduce sensitivity. There is now special antifouling; smear on a very thin layer. Trailerboat and other small boat fishermen rarely encounter marine growth such as barnacles on the transducer face.

ABOUT FISH FINDER INTERFERENCE

If your fish finder has interference, see chapter 2 for noise identification. Noise can also come from other electrical equipment and the outboard engine. This can show up as display blank outs, random targets or stray pixels, lines on the display, and no key functions. In some cases two fish finders may be running at the same time. Two boats in close proximity may cause mutual interference if using similar acoustic frequencies. If you are running two fish finders, they need to have frequencies at least 20kHz apart. If the interference is present with all systems off, the fish finder automatic noise rejection facility maybe malfunctioning. Zercom have overcome the interference from other fish finders by having dual frequency sounders between the front and rear. Vexilar have what is called the S-Cable which attenuates the power output. The power output is reduced by 70%. This is used in shallow or weed areas. The sensitivity usually has to be decreased as the power output is too high for the shallow depths. This allows two stages of gain reduction, one on power output and one for the unit. In some cases the sounder will have to be connected to a different battery to that being charged, in systems using series connections for 24 or 36 volts connect to the same battery with other circuits connected. Sometimes interference will start as outboard spark plugs degrade. The majority of outboard engines have resistor type spark plugs fitted. On some boats the tachometer is the cause of the interference. This should be disconnected at the engine to verify, and may require rerouting cables. The charging system is also a possible cause to check out. When the sounder has a filter, make sure this is selected to <ON>.

TROUBLESHOOTING FISH FINDERS AND SOUNDERS

Troubleshooting entails reading the manual and determining whether settings are correct and operating procedures are also correct. Go into the settings or options menu and ensure settings are on auto or defaulting to the factory settings.

The sounder will not start up

This is generally caused by loss of supply. Check supply switches and fuses. Check any supply circuit connections. Check that plug is properly inserted, and also that the pins are not damaged or broken. Check supply cables for damage. Look for cable nicks or cuts. If all is found to be okay with power checked at plug, the sounder switch is faulty. Use caution when straightening bent pins, they break easily. Check all connectors and connector pins for damage, and make sure they are straight and not bent. When straightening the pins there is a risk of breakage as they are brittle. Connectors not properly inserted or tightened up are prone to saltwater ingress and corrosion.

The sounder freezes or has corrupted screen data

This is generally caused by interference from the trolling motor, outboard motor electric systems or some other device, such as a pump motor. It can also be caused by faulty wiring or plug connections. Check chapter 2. Check the voltage value at the plug pins, look for over and under voltages. If there is any excess length, it should be coiled in a figure eight. Do not store it anywhere close to power cables. Connection problems are the major cause, either at the supply panel, or at the battery. Check the power at the plug using a multimeter set, with engine on or off. If the engine voltmeter shows normal charge voltages, and battery checks out, the problem is in the intermediate connections.

The sounder intermittently shuts down

This is generally caused by intermittent loss of the power supply. Check supply switches and fuses. Check any supply circuit connections. Check that plug is properly inserted, and also that the pins are not damaged or broken. Check supply cables for damage. Check that plugs are inserted properly and are not loose. It is a simple and good practice to move the cables close to connectors to identify bad connections.

The sounder has poor resolution, or range

If bottom images are poorly defined or performance has degraded, or fish do not appear to be detected, check the transducer. If the transducer is not directed straight down but is angled, this can reduce performance. Make an interference check. Check that the water depth you are fishing in is within the sounders nominal depth range. Make sure the power supply is correct, lower voltages due to poor connections or low battery can affect the unit. If the transducer is the inboard type, check that this has not deteriorated. Make some water surrounds the transducer to displace any air bubbles that may have formed.

There is an incorrect depth reading

Always check that the transducer is at the proper down angle. Check that you are not getting cavitation on the transducer head. Make sure you have the offset correctly set where this is required. In deep drafted boats you need to allow for the difference between the water surface level and the transducer level. If you do not the reading will be shallower than it actually is. Check the transducer cables for damage.

The display is either too dark or to light

Always try adjusting screen contrast and brightness controls. In general you have to alter it to suit your daylight conditions. Also vary the adjustment angle. If a screen is facing directly into the sun, the internal screen temperature rises above nominal values and goes black, so you may have to cover it and allow it to cool down.

The sounder is not marking any fish

Check that all controls are set correctly, recheck the sensitivity or gain settings, and increase the setting. Check the chart speed settings. Take it back to auto mode and select the filter if fitted to off. Check that the range of the sounder covers the depth range. Check that sounder is not set in simulator mode. The fish air bladder partly determines the display image size. Some larger fish may have small bladders and may show up small, or not at all depending on the sounder settings. Check the contrast settings, and increase to see if this improves any images. Boat movement may also affect readings. Turn the filter off if installed, and increase the transmit power setting if this function is fitted. The sounder can only mark fish that have been passed over, those at the fringes or outside the cone may not show up. Fish at the bottom may also blend in with the structure image. Always check that transom transducers have not kicked up.

Losing bottom reading at higher speeds

At higher speeds the boat hull may be coming out of the water, and so does the transducer. Often at higher speeds air bubbles are created causing cavitation and turbulence and these affect the transducer head. Transom units are commonly inaccurate at higher speeds. It is always a good practice to either reboot the set or reset to factory default settings and auto mode to verify sounder function. Noise from the outboard charging system can also cause some problems.

Why aren't the fish arching?

If the fish are not arching properly or are giving partial arches, there are a number of causes. The transducer must be mounted or oriented properly. If the angle has altered arches will not be displayed. The transducer must also be oriented correctly, in the fore and aft position. The boat speed may not be correct to form an arch, usually speed is too fast. The fish type may affect the arch formation. Some fish have different bladder sizes to others. Try increasing sensitivity or gain setting. Turn the noise filter off if installed. Increase the transmit power setting if installed. Set the contrast to a higher setting. A fish must move through the center of the cone to arch perfectly. It is also useful to go into manual mode, and adjust for a reduced vertical water column range.

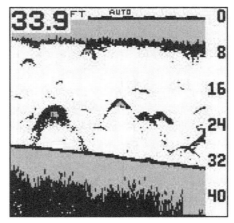

FISH ARCHING ON SCREEN
Courtesy Lowrance

ABOUT BOAT SPEED TRANSDUCERS

The boat speed transducer measures speed through the water and the GPS speed is speed over the ground. If the arm or tubes are bent or damaged the readings will be inaccurate. Boat speed readings are also affected by current, wind and course stability. All speed transducers require water without turbulence to be accurate. The speed transducers must be properly installed. Paddlewheels must be installed so that they are correctly aligned in a forward direction. Transducers are commonly fouled with weed and must be kept clean.

ABOUT UNDERWATER CAMERAS

You will have seen those great fish-cam shots on ESPN and they are now affordable for small boat fishermen. The black and white charge coupled device cameras (B and W CCD) are used for low-light applications when going below around 150 feet. The main manufacturers include Fisheye, Strike Vision, AquaVu, FishCam, SeaView. Cameras are plug and play items. Plug in the camera to the monitor and clean power supply. The 12-volt monitor and camera use power and you must consider this when planning your power system. They can be deployed and operated in a number of operational modes. Modes include drifting on the end of a downrigger wire, on a telescoping pole, or mounted on a trolling motor. It can also be used on a high-speed tow when trolling.

UNDERWATER CAMERA TECHNICAL DATA

Buying decisions include consideration of the lens angles such as wide angle; the line resolution (380, 400 etc); auto gain control and auto shutter control; minimum light levels and angles; field of vision 85, 95 degrees; cable specifications and standards. Camera housing seals are generally very robust. I spent some time as a diving technician on oil rigs and I must say you have to be very careful when reassembling housings. If they don't seal the camera properly it will soon flood. Fish Cam has the capability to add information to recordings including navigation and position information, water temperature, depth, speed through a serial data interface. The power consumption for color and black and white systems is typically 100 mA without lights and 300 mA with lights. The RCA video output is EIA/NTSC (North America) or CCIR/PAL (Europe).

9

VHF AND DSC RADIO

ABOUT VHF RADIO

Many saltwater fishermen invest in a VHF radio, either a fixed unit or a portable handheld unit. If you fish in areas where there is plenty of commercial harbor and river traffic, this may make a good investment in safety. The disadvantage is that range is line of sight, typically around 5–15 nm on small boats. There are also licensing regulations that must be adhered to and failure to comply may result in prosecution and fines. All VHF installations must possess a station license issued by the FCC or in other countries the relevant authority. When issued a call sign is also given. The person registering the installation should possess an operator's license or certificate of a one day or evening course. Cell phones are very useful but when you venture into large bays or offshore they are not a substitute for VHF. The range is less, rescuers cannot position fix on the transmission, and aircraft and SAR vessels cannot talk to you. Don't use VHF as walkie-talkies, the new FRS radios such as the Motorola Talkabout are best for this.

HOW DOES THE VHF RADIO WORK?

The VHF radio spectrum consists of 55 channels in the 156–163 MHz band. VHF is line of sight, the higher the two antennas are mounted, the greater the distance. There are theoretical ways to work out this. Factors such as atmospheric conditions and the installation itself also affect the actual range.

HOW MUCH POWER DOES VHF USE?

Typically 5–6 amps consumption on transmit. Reception is in the range of 1 to 2 amps. In a day, that can add up to 12–17 amp-hours depending on the set.

HOW TO USE A VHF RADIO

As VHF is used by official and commercial operators, it is essential to use your set properly for optimum performance.

- **Power Setting.** Always use the 1-watt low power setting for local communications, and the 25-watt high power for distance contacts.
- **Squelch Setting.** Squelch reduces the inherent background noise in the radio. Do not reduce the squelch too far, or you may suppress radio signals.
- **Simplex and Duplex.** Simplex means that talk is carried out on one frequency. Duplex is where transmit and receive are on two separate frequencies.
- **Dual Watch.** This facility enables continuous monitoring on Channel 16 and the selected channel.
- **Talk Technique.** Hold the microphone clear of the mouth approximately 2 inches and speak at a volume only slightly louder than normal. Be clear and concise and don't waste words. Many newer sets also incorporate noise-canceling microphones.

WHAT IS DSC VHF RADIO?

The saltwater fisherman who ventures offshore will be looking at the introduction of Digital Selective Calling (DSC) VHF radios. I have a Standard Horizon model on my boat. These are part of the Global Maritime Distress and Safety System or GMDSS. Channel 70 is reserved for DSC use. DSC has the advantage that digital signals in radio communications are more efficient than voice transmissions, as well as significantly faster. A DSC VHF transmission typically takes around a second to broadcast boat details and precise position. A dedicated DSC watch receiver is required to continuously monitor the specified

DSC distress frequency. Class D controllers are available from Standard Horizon, Raymarine, ICS, Icom and Simrad. DSC radios enable the transmission of digital information based on four priority groupings: Distress, Urgency, Safety, and Routine. To perform this selective transmission and reception of messages, every station must possess what is called a Maritime Mobile Selective-call Identity Code (MMSI). The DSC Distress alert message is configured to contain the transmitting vessel identity (the MMSI code or Unique Identifier Number), the time, the nature of the distress, and the vessel position where interfaced with a GPS. After transmission of a distress alert, it is repeated a few seconds later to ensure that the transmission is successful.

ABOUT VHF AERIALS

The majority of trailer boats use omni-directional whip aerials, which give maximum signal radiation distance. The aerial length is directly related to the aerial gain, and the higher the gain, the narrower the transmission beam. The fiberglass whip effectively increases the height, and therefore the range of the radiating element. There are two power ratings, one is called the effective radiated power (EP) which is the power radiated out from the antenna. The other is the true power which exists at the radio antenna connection, either 1 or 25 watts.

TROUBLESHOOTING THE VHF RADIO INSTALLATION

Damaged or cut ground shield is common where the cable has been jointed, or badly terminated at the connector. Make sure the shield is properly prepared and installed. The most common problem is badly installed or assembled connectors. The connectors must be properly tightened, the pins properly inserted, and the pin-to-cable solder joint must be sound. Dielectric faults occur when cables are run tightly around corners, through decks and bulkheads, and through cable glands. Make sure that cables are bent with a large radius, the tighter the bend, the more dielectric narrowing that will occur with increased reflected power. Pinched cables are a problem where a cable has not been properly passed through a deck with the gland or connector crushing the cable and reducing the dielectric diameter. Radio waves pass along the outside of the central core and along the inner side of the braiding. Any deformation will alter the inductance and reduce power output. Ensure that shield seals are properly made.

If an antenna has suffered damage, or if a new antenna has been damaged in transit, functional efficiency will decrease and losses increase. Inspect the antenna and connectors regularly. I always wrap the aerial connection with self-amalgamating tape to reduce ingress of water and moisture and salt air. This is the greatest cause of failure.

DSC RADIO
Courtesy Standard Horizon

VHF FREQUENCIES

United States—Great Lakes—Canada—St Lawrence. Calling, Distress, Safety is Channel 16. In US calling is on 09, but not in Canada. Recreational Channels 68–69 71–72 78 and Canada main channel is 68. Public correspondence channels in US 24–28, 84–87; in Canada 1–3, 23–28, 60, 64, 84–88. Locks, canals, bridges 13. St Lawrence Seaway Canada is 11–14. SAR in US and Canada is 22A. Weather is continuous on WX1–WX9. In Canada Great Lakes, Atlantic Coast (WX4), (WX9) and Pacific Coast (WX4), (WX1). USCG (WX) is at various times on Channel 22A. Selected areas are Buffalo (0255, 1455); South Amherst/Lorain (Ch 17 0002, 1102, 1702, 2302); Detroit 26, 28 (Ch

22 0135, 1335); Grand Haven (Ch 22 0235, 1435); Milwaukee (Ch 22 0255, 1455); Sault Sainte Marie 26 (Ch 22 0005, 1205).

Gulf of Mexico. WLO on Ch 25, 28, 84, 87 with traffic lists on the hour. St Petersburg (Ch 22 1300, 2300); Mobile 26 (Ch 22 1020, 12220, 1620, 2220); New Orleans 24, 26, 27, 87 (Ch 22 1035, 1235, 1635, 2235); Galveston 25, 86, 87 (Ch 22 1050, 1250, 1650, 2250); Corpus Christi 26, 28 (Ch 22 1040, 1240, 1640, 2240).

Atlantic Coast. Southwest Harbor 28 (WX Ch 22 1135, 2335); Portland 24, 28 (WX Ch 22 1105, 2305); Boston 26, 27 (WX Ch 22 1035, 2235); Woods Hole (WX Ch 22 1005, 2205); Long Island Sound (WX Ch 22 1120, 2320); Moriches (WX Ch 22 0020, 1220); New York 25, 26, 84 (WX Ch 22 1050, 2250); Sandy Hook 24 (WX Ch 22 1020, 2220); Cape May (WX Ch 22 1103, 2303); Baltimore 24 (WX Ch 22 0130, 1205); Charleston 26 (WX Ch 22 1200, 2200); Miami 24, 25 (WX Ch 22 1230, 2230); Key West 24, 84 (WX Ch 22 1200, 2200).

Pacific Coast. Seattle 25, 26 (WX Ch 22 CG 0630, 1830); Astoria 24, 26 (Wx Ch 22 CG 053, 1733); Portland (WX Ch 22 CG 1745); Humboldt Bay (WX Ch 22 CG 1615, 2315); San Francisco 26, 84, 87, Monterey 28 (WX Ch 22 CG 1615, 2345); Long Beach (WX Ch 22 CG 0203, 1803); San Diego 28, 86 (WX Ch 22 CG 0103, 1703). Vancouver 26 Van Inlet, Barry Inlet, Rose Inlet, Holberg, Port Hardy, Alert Bay, Eliza Dome, Cape Lazo, Watts Pt, Lulu Is, Mt Parke, Port Alberni Ch 26 Dundas, My Hayes, Klemtu, Cumshewa, Naden Harbour, Calvert, Nootka, Mt Helmcken, Mt Newton, Bowen Is, Texada, Discovery Mt Ch 84.

United Kingdom. Gale and strong wind warnings on receipt and every 2 hours. MSI transmitted for Southern Region at 0733 and 1933 on N. Foreland, Humber, Start Point 26 Orfordness, Pendennis 62 Thames 02 (0810, 2010); Hastings, Bacton, 07 Niton 28 Weymouth, Ifracombe 05 Lands End, Grimsby 27 Lands End (Scilly Is) 64 Celtic 24. Northern Region at 0703 and 1903 for Wick, Cromarty 28 Shetland, Portpatrick 27 Orkney, Stonehaven, Cullercoats, Anglesey, Clyde 26 (0820, 2020); Buchan, Whitby, Islay 25 Forth, Skye 24. HMCG broadcast MSI on Ch 26 and 83; HMCG Falmouth 26, 83 (0940, 2140); Dover 26, 83 (0940, 2140); Solent 26, 83 (0840, 2040).

New Zealand. Kaitaia 71 Whangarei 67 Great Barrier Is 68, 71 Auckland 71 Plenty 68 Runaway 71 Tolaga 67 Napier 68 Taranaki 67 Wairarapa 67 Wellington 71 Picton 68 Farewell 68 D'Urville 67 Kaikoura 67; Westport 71; Greymouth 68; Akaroa 68; Fox 67; Waitaki 67 Fiordland 71 Chalmers 71 Bluff 68 Puysegur 67.

Australia. VHF 16 for distress and safety, weather Ch 67. NSW: (WX 0648 1818) Hawkesbury 02, Camden Haven 62, Coffs Hbr 27, Eden 86. (WX 67 at 0733 and 1733 hrs EST) Sydney, Newcastle and Pt Kembla NT: (WX 0803 1833) Gove 28. QLD: (WX 0633 1633) Port Clinton 01, Weipa 03, Port Clinton 04, Torres Strait 26, Bundaberg, Cairns, Gladstone 27, Lockhart River; Whitsundays 28, Darnely Is; Ayr/Home Hill 60, Yeppoon, Cooktown 61, Fraser Is. 62, Prudoe Is, 65, Thursday Is, Shute Hbr, 66, Lockhart River, Whitsundays 86. SA: (WX 0748 1718) Adelaide 26, Kangaroo Is 61, Port Lincoln 27; TAS: (WX 0803 1733) Hobart 07, Devonport 28, Bruny is 27, St Marys 26. VIC: (WX 0803 1733) Melbourne 26, Wilsons Prom 60, 60, Lakes Entrance 27; WA: (WX 0633 1633) Carnarvon 24, Jurien Bay 62, Broome 28, Dampier 26, Port Headland 27, Geraldton 28.

South Africa and Namibia. Cape Town. Wx at 1333, 0948, 1748, on Ch 01, 04, 23, 25, 26, 27, 84,85 and 86. Kosi Bay 01 Sodwana Bay 03 Cape St Lucia 25 Richards Bay 28, 24 Durban 01, 26 Mazeppa Bay 28 East London 26 Pt Elizabeth 87 Kynsna 23 Albertinia 86, 03 Saldanha 27 Doringbaai 87 Port Nolloth 01 Alexander Bay 04 Walvis Bay 16, 23, 26, 27.

10

GPS, CHARTS, RADAR, AUTOPILOTS

WHAT IS GPS?

The US Department of Defense (DOD) operates the NAVSTAR system. The system consists of 24 satellites placed in six polar orbits, so that at least four will always be visible above the horizon at any time. GPS position fixing involves the use of a mathematical principle called trilateration. The receiver calculates a position from a number of satellites. This requires satellite ranging to measure the distance from the satellites, accurate time measurement, the location of all satellites, and correction factors for ionosphere conditions.

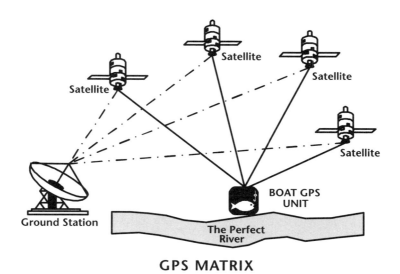

GPS MATRIX

HOW DOES A GPS OPERATE?

Turning the power initializes with the closest satellite and ephemeris data being downloaded into memory. A period of at least 20 minutes is often required to stabilize a position and verify the status of satellites, availability, etc. After switching off a GPS, the last position is retained in memory. If your position remains within 50nm, prior to the next power up, a position will generally be available within approximately 3–5 minutes. The receiver collects data from other satellites in view. After acquisition of data it locks on to a satellite to commence the ranging process. Based on the data on positions and times the receiver calculates a position solution and displays this on the screen.

Courtesy Raymarine

Courtesy Standard Horizon

GPS UNITS

WHAT IS DIFFERENTIAL GPS?

This system was developed by the U.S. Coast Guard to improve GPS accuracy levels to within 10 meters. The system uses a land-based, fixed position station that calculates theoretically correct distance and signal travel times between the station and each satellite and any errors, such as SA. The required error correction factors are then transmitted by HF radio to all mobile GPS receivers in the area with beacon receivers. This correction signal is applied to the position measurement solution of the GPS.

WHAT IS WIDE AREA AUGMENTATION SYSTEM (WAAS)?

This new and still experimental system is being developed by the US FAA for aviation. The system operates using 25 ground reference stations. Each receives GPS signals and determines any errors. Two master stations process this data and upload a correction signal to a geostationary satellite. This is rebroadcast back again to WAAS enabled GPS receivers. The accuracy is typically 15–20 ft (5–7m). As the satellite is located above the equator users may experience some blocking of WAAS in some terrain such as wooded areas. WAAS enabled GPS can give you very precise fishing coordinate accuracy better than 3 meters, 95% of the time.

HOW ACCURATE IS GPS?

The accuracy of GPS is important when the best fishing location of all time is to be returned to. The Precise Positioning Service (PPS) is primarily for military use and is derived from the Precise (P) code. The P code is transmitted on the L1 (1575.42MHz) and L2 (1227.60MHz) frequencies. PPS fixes are generally accurate within 16 meters spherical error. The Standard Positioning Service (SPS) is for civilian use and is derived from the Course and Acquisition (C/A) code.

WHAT IS SELECTIVE AVAILABILITY (SA)?

This is the process of degrading positional accuracy by altering or introducing errors in the clock data and satellite ephemeris data. SA is characterized by a wandering position, and often a course and speed over the ground of up to 1.5 knots while actually stationary. SA was officially switched off. However it is possible to be activated in times of defense emergencies. Effective May 2, 2000 selective availability has been eliminated.

WHAT IS DILUTION OF POSITION (DOP)?

Accuracy quality is quantified by what is called (Geometric) Dilution of Precision (DOP), which indicates the dilution of position precision.

The cause is poor satellite geometry or poor satellite distribution. It is generally measured on a scale of one to 10. The higher the number, the poorer the position confidence level, the lower the number the better the fix quality. There is also Horizontal Dilution of Position (HDOP), and Position DOP.

WHAT CAUSES GPS ERROR?

The GPS has inherent errors that decrease accuracy. There are GPS clock errors. Each GPS satellite has two atomic clocks which are monitored against terrestrial atomic clocks. Based on this information, the entire GPS system is continually calibrated against UTC. There are ionosphere or space weather effects. Like radio signals, both ionosphere and troposphere conditions can affect GPS accuracy. Errors occur in signal transmission times that can impose signal propagation delays. This signal refraction introduces timing errors that cause positional inaccuracies. Like radio propagation, it alters given changes in atmospheric conditions, solar activity, etc. Errors can be as great as 20–30 meters during the day and 5 meters at night. There is the Multipath Effect which occurs when signals from a satellite travelling to a receiver arrive at slightly different times due to reflection or alteration. The effect is that positions may be derived off the "bad" signal, resulting in an inaccuracy. Finally there is satellite integrity where the signal being transmitted from a satellite is corrupt due to a malfunction.

GPS SATELLITE ACQUISITION MODES

Parallel Channel. The parallel channel multiple-receiver units are now virtually standard. This enables the continuous monitoring and tracking of up to 12 satellites and the parallel processing of all those satellites in view simultaneously. These units increase position accuracy, reduce errors, and improve the HDOP.

Multiplex Receiver. Multiplex systems use one or two channels to sequentially handle satellites at high processing speeds. They are sometimes referred to as pseudo-multi-channel systems because performance under ideal conditions is nearly as fast and accurate as that of true multiple-channel systems.

ABOUT GPS INSTALLATION

Aerials should be mounted clear of fly bridge and tuna tower frames, deck equipment and other radio aerials. Where possible the aerial should have as wide a field of view as practicable, while being located as low as possible. In installations that have a tower with mounted radar, make sure that the GPS aerial is not within the radar antenna beam spread.

GPS CABLING

Power supply cables should be routed as far as practicable from equipment cables carrying high currents. Aerial cables should also be routed well clear. It is extremely important for the aerial cable not to be kinked, bent, or placed in any tight bend radius. This has the effect of narrowing the dielectric gap within the coaxial cable, which may cause signal problems. Make sure all through-deck glands are high quality and properly protect the cable. Do not shorten or lengthen an aerial cable unless your manufacturer approves it.

GPS CONNECTORS

Make sure that all connectors are properly inserted into the GPS receiver. Ensure that screw-retaining rings are tight, because plugs can work loose and cause intermittent contact. The coaxial connector from the aerial into the receiver should be rotated properly so that it is locked in. External aerial connections should be made water-resistant where possible. Use of self-amalgamating tape is a good method for doing this. If you have to remove and refit an aerial connector, use considerable care and assemble the connector in accordance with the manufacturer's instructions.

GROUNDING THE GPS

The ground connection provided with the system must be connected to the RF ground system or negative supply polarity depending on manufacturer's recommendations. On aluminum boats this is the hull.

ABOUT GPS POWER SUPPLIES

A clean power supply is essential to proper operation. Use either an in-line filter or install suppressors across noisy motors and alternator. The power supply should not come from a battery used for engine starting, or used with any high current equipment such as the trolling motor.

TROUBLESHOOTING THE GPS

The GPS has a large fix error
The GPS system may be down, or a satellite may be shut down. Check your navigation information source for news of outages. The HDOP may simply be excessive due to poor satellite geometry in your location. With sequential receivers, loss of signal may be a problem in heavy sea states. For fishermen in inland river areas, satellite shadowing can occur from forest and timber to steep cliff and bank faces.

The GPS has a small fix error
Errors that are not large but consistently outside normal accuracy levels are due to a number of sources. The signal may be subject to an excessive amount of atmospheric disturbances, such as periods of extensive solar flare activity. The aerial connections and part of the installation may have degraded, so check the entire system. Make sure aerial is vertical and not partially pushed over in fixed installations. In many handheld cases it is best to get proper brackets and keep them vertical.

The GPS has no position fix
This is often caused by a total loss of a satellite view or when a satellite goes out of service. Another common cause is the aerial being pushed over to horizontal, so check that it is vertical in fixed installations. Handheld users should make sure that the unit is in a clear position with aerial vertical. Aerial damage after being struck by equipment is a cause of a sudden fix loss. Check all cables and connections. If these show no defects, a check of all initialization parameters may be necessary; if those check out, the receiver and aerial may require manufacturer servicing.

The GPS data is corrupted

This error can be caused by power supply problems. Check whether this coincides with trolling motor or outboard run periods. Radiated interference is also a possibility, often from other radio equipment such as a cell phone or VHF. Another quite common cause of data corruption is that caused by "fingers." Has another person unfamiliar with operating the GPS altered configuration parameters such as time settings or altitude? This happens quite often. It is good practice to have the basic operating instructions on a plasticized card.

ABOUT ELECTRONIC CHART PLOTTING

The GPS and electronic chart have merged and are being increasingly used by many fishermen. A Raster Chart is identical to the paper chart, and originates from original government master charts. The scanning of paper charts to create a raster image produces a vector chart. These are then vectorized to store data in layers, which allows easy zooming in on detail. They do not resemble conventional charts. The advantages over raster charts are much faster screen update rates. The charts are stored on solid-state memory cards that include C-Cards and PCMCIA cards. C-map have their Pro-Angler C-card series of chart cartridges. Garmin have CD-ROM charts such as Fishing Hot Spots which includes most of the US Central and Northern lakes. It gives detailed shoreline, depth contours, navigational aids, lake profiles and fishing hints. This can downloaded and viewed on some Garmin GPS units. The Lakemaster CD ROM is a multi-function lake mapping tool. It can also download information to a GPS. Each state edition gives lake contours, islands, reefs etc.

Courtesy Standard Horizon   *Courtesy C-Map*

CHART PLOTTER AND CHART CARTRIDGE

RADAR ON SMALL FISHING BOATS

Fishing boats as small as 16–17 feet now have radar installed. Radar is becoming popular with boats venturing into large bays, estuaries and near offshore. The units have small 18" radomes and 6–7" LCD high resolution displays. The radar transmits pulses of microwave, which are reflected back when they strike an object or target. The time delay between transmission and reception is processed along with the direction and strength of the returned echo to display on the screen. The radars in small boats have nominal ranges of 12–16nm. However it's important to understand that you cannot actually see this far unless it is a prominent coastline. It doesn't matter how much power output you use, you can only see 7% more than the horizon. A scanner mounted at just 6 feet can only see a target at water level of 3nm, and a 20-foot high target (such a small ship) at 8.5 nm. The higher the radar scanner the greater the range. When installing radar you must factor this into the battery power calculation. While radomes are most common, if you can install open array scanners you will benefit from a narrower beamwidth and better target resolution. Units also have automatic tuning, sensitivity and clutter control.

ABOUT RADAR PLOTTING AIDS

The whole basis of radar is to detect both stationary and moving targets. Radar has a number of basic features:

- **Range Rings.** They will alter with the selected radar range. Many have up to 12 range settings.
- **Variable Range Maker (VRM).** This function uses the range rings and the marker, and many types of radar have two VRMs. The readout appears on the screen, but as with all navigational exercises, make sure you are measuring the correct target. Many errors are made this way, which is why radar should be used in conjunction with other position keeping systems.
- **Electronic Bearing Line (EBL).** The most commonly used function in conjunction with the VRM enables easy plotting of a target. Use caution as many incidents are derived from taking a bearing without checking what display setting is in use, such as true or relative motion.

- **Target Expansion.** This function on many types of radar allows small- or long-range contacts to be expanded, and can be very useful when making landfalls of low altitude, particularly low islands.
- **Off-Centering.** A number of radar sets have an offset function. This alters the screen center (the vessel) another 50% down the screen, so that forward long-range observation is possible in the same radar range.
- **Guard Zones.** Guard zones offer real advantages in safety. They can be set for complete circular coverage or for specific sectors. However it is wrong to rely on these functions. A proper observation should be made regularly. On some radars, an economy or sleep mode saves power by letting the guard zone and alarm function operate without the screen being on.

INSTALLING AND MAINTAINING RADAR

There are some basic installation and maintenance procedures. The generally accepted warning is to place the scanner above eye level. Some say that the exposure from a rotating scanner is relatively low, but it's best to avoid the risk. Most are located on stainless steel structures. It is important to ensure that radar cables running within the tubing are properly protected at entry and exit points, as sharp edges will cut into the cables. The scanner is usually angled for the proposed use. If you drift fish or slow troll, level mounting should be okay. If it is a planing hull boat, it should be angled so that it is level when up on the plane. Once every year open the scanner and tighten all connections. Keep the scanner clean with warm and soapy water, don't use scourers or harsh detergents. Check and tighten the scanner bolts. Check that the scanner watertight gaskets are sealing properly and are clean. The final and most important check is to make sure that the connectors are tight and waterproof. Check for any signs of corrosion. Check ground wires are secure. Always place a cover over the display when not in use and remove for the winter.

AUTOPILOTS FOR TRAILERBOATS

Autopilot technology on small fishing boats is now based on powerful microprocessors and complex software algorithms that give "intelligent" control. Systems such as the Raymarine SportsPilot, Simrad, SITEX and the Teleflex Easy Pilot use common design principles. The basic function of an autopilot is to steer the boat on a predetermined and set course, compass heading or to a position or waypoint. The autopilot makes course corrections in proportion to the course error, and corrects the boat heading to eliminate any overshoot as the course is met. This type of control is called proportional rate. The course correction is based on the degree of course deviation and the rate of the change.

THE AUTOPILOT CONTROL SYSTEM

The type of autopilot fitted to a fishing boat varies according to the type of steering system used. Autopilots are available to suit single and twin outboard installations. The autopilot system requires a drive connected to the steering system. This can be either a push-pull cable or hydraulic steering system. The hydraulic system requires the use of a reversible DC pump that is controlled by the pilot for directional control. The Raymarine RaySports control fastens behind the steering wheel. The system has a Central Processing Unit (CPU) that inputs heading and position data. It then outputs control commands to the steering system. The heading data comes from a fluxgate compass. The control head or display unit is used to activate the pilot, display heading or feedback data, navigation data and alarms. There are also hand control systems. Rate Gyro compasses allow rapid real time sensing of vessel yawing that is prevalent in lightweight vessels. This data input is supplemental to the fluxgate signal and allows quick correction to counter the rapidly altering heading changes that cannot be compensated for by the fluxgate. An NMEA 0183 (or SeaTalk with Raymarine) allows input from a GPS so that steering to a position or waypoint is possible.

ABOUT AUTOPILOT OPERATION

Many adjustments can be made to achieve optimum autopilot operation. Most pilots have automatic sea state and trim functions.

- **Deadband.** This is the area in which the heading can deviate or yaw before the pilot initiates a correction. It varies with sea state conditions.
- **Gain.** This is related to the amount of rudder (outboard turning) to be applied for the detected heading error, and must be calibrated. This factor is linked to proper compass setup and damping. When gain is set too low the correction response is slow to return to set heading. When the gain is too high the course oscillates (yaws) around the set heading. When excessive gain is used the course is unstable with gradual increases in heading error and course. Most systems have several sensitivity settings as well as settings for high and low speeds.
- **Feedback.** The feedback reference provides the precise instantaneous outboard position information to the autopilot. It is essential that the feedback sensor be properly aligned. Pilots have a high-resolution potentiometer linear or rotary feedback unit.
- **Warning.** Do not use the autopilot in any channels, confined areas or heavy traffic zones. Don't use a cellular telephone or handheld VHF close to the autopilot as operation can interfere and cause sudden course changes.

INSTALLING AND TROUBLESHOOTING AUTOPILOTS

The majority of autopilot problems occur due to improper selection, incorrect installation, or improper operation. Make sure that system components are not exposed to excessive saltwater and seals are intact. Ingress of water is a common failure mode. Regularly check plugs and sockets for water and moisture. Make sure that they seal properly. When cleaning use a damp cloth. Do not use solvents or abrasive materials. Do not use a high-pressure hose. If the outboard suddenly drives hard over, check for radio interference (cell phone/VHF), loss of feedback signal, fluxgate compass failure, GPS data corruption or control unit failure. An unstable wandering course is due to incorrect calibration, over damped compass, rudder gain setting incorrect, feedback transducer, control unit fault or a drive unit fault. The accuracy of fluxgate or solid state gyro compass can be influenced by placing magnetic objects next to them. Make sure the area is clear.

ALL ABOUT EPIRBS

Many smaller trailer boats venturing offshore should also have an Emergency Position Indicating Radio Beacon (EPIRB). GMDSS incorporates the COSPAS/SARSAT system as an integral part of the distress communications system. The acronym is based on the former Soviet "Space System for Search of Distress Vessels" and the American "Search and Rescue Satellite Aided Tracking." The system is a worldwide satellite-assisted SAR system for location of distress transmissions emitted by Class B (121.5 MHz) and 406 MHz EPIRB frequencies, 406 MHz units also have the 121.5 MHz frequency. 121.5 kHz is an aircraft homing frequency that enables aircraft to assist in SAR operations. The 406 MHz units have a unique identification code, and information is programmed at time of sale, with a unique Identifier Number. You must register the EPIRB unit properly and provide all of the appropriate data. Man Overboard (MOB) locators come as wristwatch and small PFD units and have small ranges and battery life. A Personal Locator Beacon (PLB) is a small GPS enabled 406 MHz EPIRB and has reduced size batteries.

ABOUT THE EPIRB ACTIVATION SEQUENCE

Do not operate an EPIRB except in a real emergency. Do not even operate it for just a short period of time and then switch it off. Authorities may assume your vessel went down quickly before circumstances stopped transmission.

1. The EPIRB transmits, the 406 MHz has coded information and GPS units include the precise position.
2. A satellite detects the distress transmission and determines the location. For 406 MHz units this is within 1nm.
3. The detected signal retransmits to a ground station (LUT).
4. The LUT sends the distress information to a Mission Control

Center (MCC) before going to a Rescue Control Center (RCC) and then to SAR aircraft and vessels. These use the 121.5 MHz homing signal to locate the boat.

There is a time lag from detection of a signal and physical location. The 121.5 MHz has a 6-hour time lag to notification, the 406 MHz has a 1-hour average. A 406 MHz with GPS is just 5 minutes. Every LUT has a "footprint" coverage area, and the closer you are to the edge of that footprint, the longer the delay. If you have to activate, be patient and wait.

Acknowledgements

Thanks and appreciation to the following companies and organizations for their assistance. Readers should contact them for advice and supply. Quality equipment is part of reliability!

BoatUS Trailering Magazine (Pat Piper)   www.boatus.com
Ranger Boats   www.rangerboats.com
Lowrance(Steve Wegrzyn)   www.lowrance.com
Bassmaster   www.bassmaster.com
NAFC (Join today)   www.nafc.com
Blue Seas   www.bluesea.com
Standard Horizon (Terry Crockett)   www.standardhorizon.com
Motorguide   www.motorguide.com
Big Jon   www.bigjon.com
Cannon   www.cannon.com
BassPro   www.basspro-shops.com
DualPro   www.dualpro.com
Cabela's   www.cabelas.com
Minn Kota   www.minnkotamotor.com
ANCOR   www.ancorproducts.com
AC Delco   www.acdelco.com
Guest   www.guestco.com
Hellroaring   www.hellroaring.com
Humminbird   www.humminbird.com
Outboard Electric   www.outboardelectric.org
PinPoint Fishing   www.pinpointfishing.com
ProTroll   www.protroll.com
Penn   www.pennreels.com
Raymarine   www.raymarine.com
Simrad   www.simrad.com
Scotty   www.scottyusa.com
Trolling Thunder   www.hepi.com
Vexilar   www.vexilar.com
Zercom   www.zercom.com

Index